# BEHIND THE
# THERAPISTS'
# NOTES

## —Fears, Feelings, and Hopes—

## ABOUT THE AUTHOR

Dr. Kent is listed in *Who's Who in the West* and in *Who's Who in the World*. He has a B.A. from Yale and graduate degrees from Columbia, Mills, University of Southern California, and Johannes Gutenberg University.

In addition to his years in private practice, Dr. Kent served as Chief Psychologist, USAF Wiesbaden Hospital; Head of the Department of Behavioral Science, University of Southern Colorado, and Director of Mental Health, Indian Health Service at the Quechan and Cocopah Reservations. Dr. Kent is a Diplomate in Clinical Psychology and a Fellow of the America Psychological Association.

Dr. Kent is the author of: *A Psychologist Answers Your Questions; Conflict Resolution;* and *Three Warriors Against Substance Abuse.*

# BEHIND THE THERAPISTS' NOTES

## —Fears, Feelings, and Hopes—

THEODORE C. KENT

First Edition

Library of Congress Catalog No. 92-72426
Copyright © 1993 by Theodore C. Kent

Libra Publishers, Inc.
3089C Clairemont Drive, Suite 383
San Diego, CA 92117

Manufactured in the United States of America

ISBN 0-87212-256-5

All names of persons, places, events and circumstances in these narratives are fictitious. The narrators do not exist as individuals. They are composites of actual people who are unidentifiable. Except for a few large cities and states, geographical names of places are also fictitious. I could find no "Glenville" in any list of cities in Texas. Any resemblance to names of real people and places is entirely coincidental. However, all symptoms and descriptions of mental conditions are clinically accurate and may be found in the *Diagnostic and Statistical Manual of Mental Disorders (Third Edition–Revised)*. Washington, D.C.: American Psychiatric Association, 1987.

Theodore C. Kent, Ph.D.

# DEDICATION

To my sister, Margaret, whose professional career as a social worker was devoted to helping children.

# CONTENTS

# FOREWORD

The notes that I take in my office when I sit across the desk from my clients enable me later to piece together comprehensive pictures of their mental and emotional conditions. Those I use to record their progress in therapy contain more clinically useful information than the narrators of this book divulge in their absorbing accounts of their problems. However, unless a reader is a professional in the mental health field, clinical notes do not communicate deeper feelings, anxieties, fears, and hopes in the full flavor of their personal reality as the narrators have done in Dr. Kent's book.

Years ago, just after I had finished my training in clinical psychology, one of my first clients had a problem that was severely distressing. I was delighted that I had been sufficiently perceptive to have provided the right intervention required for his recovery. Imagine my surprise when I learned in our final session that a casual remark I had made in a long-forgotten session had been the turning point for him.

Over the years I have come to appreciate surprises in therapy as a confirmation of the flexibility and potentiality of the human psyche. Both the drama of the clients' dilemmas and the unexpected outcomes of therapies that sometimes occur are represented and felicitously combined in *Behind the Therapists' Notes*. Fault cannot be found with the work from the point of clinical accuracy.

Dr. Kent has written a thought-provoking book that offers the reader an opportunity to experience vicariously the narrators' feelings and relate to what they endured. I am inclined to think that the reader will benefit from the reading as I have.

William J. Matulich, Ph.D.
Consulting Psychologist
San Diego, California

# ACKNOWLEDGEMENTS

I thank my wife, Shirley, for making suggestions and editing *Behind the Therapists' Notes*, and thank Pat Yates for contributing her editing and computer skills to help ready the book for publication. I appreciate Dr. Eva B. McCullars' insightful comment following Ralph's narrative.

It has been a delight to work with Libra Publishers. Many thanks to Darryl DiRuscio for designing the cover and the book.

# INTRODUCTION

People coping with emotional problems sometimes live behind walls of psychological evaluations, psychiatric diagnoses, and even superstitions.

In the pages of this book you will meet people with emotional problems under different circumstances. They will tell you their story from their own perspectives. As they share their experiences with you, they reveal their very personal fears, feelings, and hopes. The ironic twists and unexpected outcomes of some of the therapies described in the book may be thought-provoking and, perhaps, controversial. However, all of the narrators' symptoms and diagnoses are clinically accurate.

The narrators represent a composite of clients from a variety of mental health sources. The spectrum of situations in the book fits into the agenda of an eclectic mental health practice, and reflects current social/mental health concerns.

As you turn the pages of this book, it may occur to you as it has to me, that in the deep sense of being human we are all sisters and brothers. Then we may recognize unexpected similarities between ourselves and the storytellers. As we look behind the therapists' notes and read what the narrators reveal about themselves, the truth may strike us with full force—''there, but for the grace of God, go I!''

T. C. K.

# BEHIND THE THERAPISTS' NOTES

## —Fears, Feelings, and Hopes—

*It seems incredible that anyone could have an uncontrollable urge to expose his genitals to a stranger. But in spite of the danger of getting caught, there are men who yield to their recurrent, intense, sexual urges to expose themselves to an unsuspecting female. Called exhibitionism, the condition isn't easy to cure. But one never knows what a little old lady may do to help out—if she's had the right kind of experiences, of course!*

# PETE:
# What a Little Old Lady Saw

My name is Pete. It was only a few years back that I seriously considered taking my own life. After thinking about it for a while, I decided that I didn't deserve to die because the ideas that possessed me always forced their way into my mind against my will.

Back in high school was the first time I gave in to an overwhelming urge to expose my genitals to a girl. Even in those days I knew that this urge wasn't normal. Seeing a girl's face turning away in shock released all kinds of built-up tensions within me. Not until I had exposed myself and stimulated myself to orgasm was the terrible restlessness within me stilled—at least for a while.

I recall the first time it happened. I was sixteen years old. My mother had died the year before, and I lived with my father and older brother. One day I walked home from school with a shy, blond girl who lived next door but wasn't a special friend. Her family was very religious and didn't allow her to go to dances or date. On the way home I convinced her to take a shortcut through a back alley. While we were passing through the alley, I gave in to an urge that had been building up in me. I pulled down my zipper and, without saying a word, exposed my genitals to her.

The look of disbelief and shock on her face remains burned in my mind. I was sure that she would run home to tell her parents what had happened. When I got home I told my father what I had done rather than letting him hear about it from her parents. I tried to explain it by saying I must be crazy. I expected to get a severe scolding or worse. Instead, my father only looked sorrowful and upset. He put his hand on my shoulder and told me that he would try to get me the help I obviously needed.

The police came to our house a little while later to pick me up. My father advised me to go with them quietly. They took me to the juvenile detention center where I was held until my hearing at juvenile court a few days later.

At the hearing, the judge placed me on probation and ordered me to have regular counseling sessions with a psychologist. The psychologist's name was Dr. Sanders. In our first session of therapy, I told him that an urge to expose myself sometimes overwhelmed me. Reluctantly, I admitted that it was accompanied by a strong need to masturbate. He seemed to take this in stride.

Dr. Sanders asked me to describe how I felt after I had masturbated. I told him that I felt as if the person I'd been before was drained out of me, leaving only self-hate behind. At that time I didn't understand what he meant when he remarked, ''Hate is a sandwich. Self-hate is the part that lies between invisible layers of self-love.''

In the counseling sessions that followed, even though I was ashamed, I told Dr. Sanders that I had never made love to a girl. That didn't seem to surprise him. I admitted that I really was afraid of girls and terrified at the idea of ever having sex with one. I felt better when I saw that Dr. Sanders accepted this casually and didn't act as if I were crazy.

Dr. Sanders asked me to try to recall things that had happened early in my life. In looking back, a frightening picture came to my mind. I remembered myself as a little kid masturbating in the bathroom. My mother walked in and saw what I was doing. I hadn't locked the door because I didn't expect her to come in to get a bottle of aspirin from the bathroom cabinet. When she caught sight of me she seemed shocked and became very angry. "Shame on you!" she said, shaking a finger at me. Then she threatened me, saying, "The next time I catch you abusing yourself, I'll cut your pecker off!" For a long time after that I didn't even dare to look at my genitals, much less touch them.

One day on my way home from school, I saw a boy about my age urinating against the wall of a house. I wondered what my mother would say if she ever caught me doing that. That night I dreamed I was going to urinate against a house just as the boy had. In my dream, people were crowding all around to watch me. As I unzipped my pants, I looked down and saw that my sexual parts were missing! There was absolutely nothing between my legs! The people in the crowd pointed to where my genitals should have been and laughed. Above their laughter I heard a woman's mocking voice, "He doesn't have anything to do it with!"

Dr. Sanders asked me to try to remember other things that had happened to me in the past. I recalled that when I was in school I usually got good grades in all of my subjects. That used to infuriate a bully who always earned a string of F's on his report card. He used to wait for me after school and pick on me. I tried hard to avoid him, but one day he caught sight of me just as I was leaving the school yard. He ran over to block my way and gave me a hard punch in the chest.

"You leave me alone!" I yelled, and turned away from him.

"Hit me back!" he challenged, sticking out his chest for me to hit. I ran off as fast as I could and managed to get away. The pain from his punch didn't bother me as much as his calling after me, "Sissy, sissy, you ain't got what it takes!"

Dr. Sanders explained that problems involving sex usually aren't very easily corrected. He also told me that he found me resisting the therapy and that would make it harder for me to be cured. But he still seemed to have hope for me because he continued the counseling sessions. When I asked him what caused me to have the urge to expose myself, he explained that things that had happened to me made me fear that I lacked a penis. Seeing a female's look of shock when I exposed myself made it obvious to me that I really did have genitals. Only then could I feel good enough about myself to masturbate and get sexual release. Perhaps that is what Dr. Sanders meant when he'd told me earlier that self-hate is somehow mixed up with self-love.

Dr. Sanders kept trying to build up my self-esteem. He told me he was glad that I had enrolled in computer programming school. With his encouragement I joined a neighborhood social club and a young people's church group. As I gained more confidence, the urge to expose myself quieted down. After a while there came a time when it seemed that I no longer had the urge. My counseling sessions were then tapered off and, finally, terminated. When my last session with him was over, Dr. Sanders wished me luck and asked me to phone him if the urges ever returned. At my court hearing, my lawyer told the judge that I had become a "sexually normal" person, and shortly after, the judge took me off probation.

My dad was relieved to learn that the counseling had cured me, and happy that I now had friends and a social life. The day I brought a young lady home from the church group, he was delighted. He took me aside and gave me money so I could take her out for dinner at one of the best restaurants in town.

One afternoon, several months after I had completed my therapy, I found myself imagining that I was exposing myself to a woman who had passed me on the street the previous day. I tried to punish myself for thinking such thoughts, and tried to get rid of them. I skipped desserts, then meals, and did painful and exhausting exercises. Nothing prevented the urge from returning, and it became stronger as time went on.

I found myself sitting next to a young woman in a movie theater not long after this. Before I could give it a second thought, I was exposing my sexual parts to her. She screamed when she saw what I was doing. Even as the police approached, I could hardly stop masturbating. This time they'll really throw the book at me, I thought, as the police took me along with them. Now I hated myself more than ever.

I was really surprised when the judge decided to give me another chance. He sentenced me to two years probation and told me to continue attending the school where I studied computer programming. The judge stipulated that I get therapy at the county mental health clinic until the mental health experts declared me cured. He warned me several times to cooperate fully with the doctors at the clinic. Otherwise, he told me, I might have to go to jail and stay there for a couple of years. He made it clear that he was giving me my last chance.

Picturing myself behind bars in a jail cell really scared me. I made up my mind that this time I would cooperate fully with anyone who tried to help me control myself. I would keep nothing back and tell them anything they wanted to know.

When I reported to the clinic, I could see immediately that they were well-organized. The intake social worker who received me had instructions for me already typed out. She told me that I would be treated by a psychiatric team and that medications would be prescribed if the psychiatrist felt they were needed. She handed me a time schedule for outpatient appointments and informed me that absences would be reported to the judge.

The therapy program consisted of several sessions of psychological testing, periodic interviews with a social worker, regularly scheduled meetings with a psychiatrist, and continuing group therapy led by a psychiatric nurse and an aide. The psychiatrist was a young-looking man who had recently finished his training. I was pleasantly surprised by his friendliness and the natural way he acted toward me. I was hopeful that after I had completed therapy this time, I would be a normal and happy person.

After months of group counseling and therapy, the urge to expose myself seemed as foreign to me as if it had occurred to someone entirely other than myself. I no longer felt self-hate. It had been replaced by a new confidence in myself.

About a year after I had started therapy at the clinic, the day came when I was asked to attend a final meeting with the group of mental health people who had worked with me. I felt secure and comfortable as I sat in the conference room while they discussed my progress. They seemed to be pleased with the results of the therapy and took turns congratulating me for having given them full cooperation. Now I only needed a few additional visits as follow-ups. When I said good-bye to the psychiatrist, he made me promise to call the clinic for an appointment if the urge to expose myself ever returned.

The judge was notified that I had completed therapy successfully. I left the clinic full of hope for the future. I felt like a man who had lived in darkness most of his life and was able to see the world in all its brightness and beauty for the first time.

It was just a couple of months later when I noticed an old lady who had previously attracted my attention from time to time. She usually came out of a side door of the church in our neighborhood. In her prim, old-fashioned clothes she looked like somebody's grandmother. A seeming sternness on her old, wrinkled face gave me the feeling that she would stand for no nonsense. Something prudish in her expression had caught my attention and excited me. It hit me that something about her, I wasn't sure what, reminded me of my mother.

People weren't worshipping at the time of day the old lady would emerge from the church side door. I guessed that she worked in the church or was a volunteer, or perhaps went there at times to pray alone.

I will never forget the day I found myself hiding in the well-tended shrubbery that partially shielded the church door from the street. When I saw the old lady coming through the door, I held my breath as my hand reached for my pants' zipper.

As she passed me, the old lady stopped to look at my exposed genitals. I could feel my heart racing as she came closer, adjusting her glasses, and looking at me in silence. Something turned within me as I saw that she remained calm. I thrust my genitals toward her, and a voice inside of me shouted, "Scream, you old bitch! Don't you see what I am doing? Scream! Scream! Scream! Call the cops!"

"Well, young man," the old lady said at last, the telltale click of false teeth clearly audible, "I've seen a lot of those during my lifetime. Been married three times and had boyfriends before that." Then, to my horror, she chuckled!

The lady continued to look at my exposed penis appraisingly. With a shock I was reminded of the judging of animals at the county fair I had attended a couple of days before. With her head tilted ever so slightly and a touch of regret in her voice, she announced, "Your dicker doesn't look different enough from all the others I've seen to win a ribbon." Then she shrugged her shoulders and shuffled away, oblivious of my indescribable turmoil.

Several years have passed. I have a good job and am delighted that my wife is pregnant, but no more so than my father is at the idea of becoming a grandfather. I am now an honored alumnus of the county mental health clinic where my case is sometimes cited as an example of the clinic's success.

Not long ago, the young psychiatrist who had been my primary therapist telephoned and invited me to his office. He asked me if I would be willing to serve as a community representative on the clinic's advisory board. There was pride in his voice as he confided, "The success our clinic has had in curing conditions like yours has helped us get sufficient funding to continue our work and expand our service."

## COMMENT:

*Exhibitionism is one of several types of sexual disorders that appear bizarre to persons not acquainted with the range and frequency of sexual dysfunctions. People not familiar with psychiatric literature usually find it difficult to imagine that some people have irresistible compulsions to act out seemingly strange sexual fantasies.*

*There are some people with abnormal sexual fantasies who can be dangerous, especially if their fantasies are accompanied by a psychotic personality component. This is one of the reasons why the general public has little tolerance for people with sexual disorders. Among persons acting on urges to expose themselves, there is no attempt at further sexual activity and, therefore, exhibitionists are not usually physically dangerous to their victims, who are almost always females—children or adult.*

*The onset of this disorder usually occurs before the age of 18, although it may begin later. Persons acting on urges to expose themselves are distressed by these urges, as Pete was. Suicidal thinking is common, but seldom acted out. Most sexual disorders tend to become chronic. One may think of them as presenting a greater than average therapeutic challenge. Behavioral therapy is currently used in working with these patients.*

*In psychoanalytic literature, exhibitionism is viewed as a castration anxiety in which the patient believes he has lost possession of his genitals as a result of fear from castration threats experienced in childhood or early youth. He exhibits himself to gain reassurance that he has a penis and then is able to give himself sexual release.*

*Of course, the little old lady wasn't solely responsible for Pete's cure. It resulted from the cumulative efforts of previous therapies. But the shock the little old lady gave Pete by her unruffled composure when he exposed himself to her may have helped bring the previous therapies to fruition at that time.*

*I am sure I needn't say that Pete's narrative wasn't intended to suggest that unflappable little old ladies be recruited as therapists for exhibitionists. But in psychotherapy one never knows what unexpected event may turn out helpful to a client.*

*Wilhelmina counted the items on the shelves in her assigned section of the drugstore over and over to be sure she had them right. ''Pay more attention to your work and less to playing number games,'' her boss had told her several times. But he was tolerant. She's overconscientious and maybe a bit crazy, he thought and shrugged—better that way than careless.*

*At the time, her boss didn't know that Wilhelmina was in therapy for a compulsive disorder. He thought, later, that her cure was worse than the disease.*

# WILHELMINA:
# Is It Locked?

It was eleven-fifteen P.M. I drew my robe over my pajamas and walked back to the front door. I checked the door again carefully and found it tightly locked. The safety bolt was securely lodged in the doorjamb. I hadn't been completely sure, although I had tested it several times before. Everything was okay. I was sure now.

My alarm was set for 5:30 A.M. As I climbed back into bed I caught a glimpse of my skinny body in the dresser mirror. I thought that if only I could get more sleep I would gain weight. In bed I took a deep breath. Before I could exhale all the way, a thought struck me, bringing near panic. Did I turn the key far enough to the right when I locked the door? I felt perspiration on my forehead. This was silly. I knew that I had locked it securely, didn't I? "Let me check it just once more—for the last time!" I pleaded, talking to myself as I climbed out of bed and walked toward the door.

I was in bed once more. Again I was uncertain. Did I lock the door tightly this time? Was I insane? I reached for the bottle of valium. It was almost empty. Dr. Welsh is a miser when it comes to valium. He's afraid that I might head into addiction. But addiction is better than the anxiety I have day and night. I took time out to imagine what it would be like to be addicted and felt relieved that I was not. It wasn't long before I was worrying again. Did I really turn the key far enough to lock the door securely?

My name is Wilhelmina. My mother's family is German and I was named after my grandfather, Wilhelm. I work in one of those modern chain drugstores that sells almost everything—medicines, socks, cameras, radios, you name it. I'm in the medicines section, not pharmaceutical, but nonprescription items—aspirin, vitamins, skin creams and so on.

Our store is one of those help-yourself kind.

Some of the employees are assigned sections for which they are responsible. They circulate, take stock, and replace the merchandise customers take from shelves and abandon far from where they picked it up. The location of the things we sell appears on large signs suspended from the ceiling above each aisle. We help people who can't find what they are looking for even when they are standing right under the sign that tells them where it is. Employees are also supposed to look out for shoplifting. It happens often enough, but I've never gotten used to reporting it. Having to do that turns my stomach. I guess I feel sorry for the people who are caught.

No one knows the location of the merchandise we sell better than I do. I can find most things quickly and I know better than anyone else where they are stocked in the back of the store. That's because I practice recalling them often, even during my lunch hour. The manager, Mr. Sommers, knows that I am very hardworking. He sees me counting things over and over to make sure that I counted correctly. One afternoon he watched as I counted bottles of men's hair dressing a half dozen times. Instead of being pleased, he told me that I was spending too much time in stocktaking. When he saw that I looked distressed by his disapproval, he added that he wished some of the others would be as conscientious as I was.

All employees are trained to work the cash registers and we take turns at the checkout counters. I like that part of the job least, because I am never sure that I have counted the money correctly. I haven't made a mistake yet, but I would feel much better if I had the chance to count the money a second or a third time. There are just too many people lined up and waiting at the cash register to do that. It really bothers me not to be sure about anything at work because I don't want to make mistakes and get fired from my job.

I have to support myself and jobs are scarce these days. I could only get part-time employment before I started working at the drugstore. I've been able to build up some longevity and am signed up for the company's retirement and medical plans. I have to look out for myself because I'm single and twenty-eight. My salary enables me to maintain a small apartment about a mile from the store and to own the three-year-old Mazda I drive to work. The pay isn't much, but it's the security that I appreciate.

"Two bottles of Vitalis are missing from the shelf in Row 4," I told Mr. Sommers. "No one paid for them at the checkout counter. They must have been stolen. It could have been one of the one hundred and thirty-two adults that walked through my toilet articles' section yesterday," I said, speaking almost as if I were a robot. "None of the twenty-three children I saw in the store that day would have any use for the Vitalis. It's a male item but we can't be sure that it was a male who took it."

"Thank you, Sherlock Holmes," my boss said. "Pay more attention to your work and less to playing number games," he added, not looking pleased.

"I'm seeing a psychologist," I blurted out, and stood frozen in shock at having admitted this. He looked at me for a moment without saying anything. Then he said, "That's covered by our revised medical insurance, Wilhelmina."

A wave of relief swept over me, followed by a surge of loyalty to him. Right then I made up my mind that I would never give Mr. Sommers any reason to regret that he had hired me. I gave him a grateful look and returned to my section of the store feeling pleasantly secure. Then I started to look for items that were in low supply. We need to reorder multivitamins, I noted. I counted the remaining bottles three times. I counted them again because I wanted to be sure.

I told Dr. Beatty, my psychologist, that except for two things, I had lived a dull and uneventful life. One of those was when I was fourteen and my sister, Anne, who is two years older than I am, got pregnant. My parents were shocked. She had a little girl. I thought the baby was so cute when she brought her home from the hospital. I remembered crying when I heard that Anne was going to put the baby up for adoption. I wanted her to give the baby to me. Anne laughed when she heard this and told me, "If you want one, get your own!" My parents were upset enough about my sister's having the baby, but what happened to me later that same year upset them almost as much.

I went to one of the larger stores in the mall with a girl I knew from my math class in school. Her name was Emmy. Sometimes she didn't do her homework and would copy mine before class. I let her do it because, outside of her, I had few friends at school. On the day that we went to the mall, Emmy told me that her grandparents had given her some money for her birthday and that she wanted to buy some clothes and other things. Emmy brought along a green cloth shopping bag. I thought that it was odd to bring a shopping bag since they usually give you a bag at the checkout counter in most stores. I wanted to look at some shoes that were on another floor of the department store and we agreed to meet outside in front of the store in about a half hour.

When I met Emmy, she was out of breath. She handed me her bag and pointed to a telephone booth across the street, saying she had to call her mother and she'd be right back. But she ran right by the phone booth and disappeared. I couldn't understand what was going on until a man and two women came out of the store, walked over to me and ordered me to open Emmy's green shopping bag, which I was holding.

"There they are!" one of the women said, pointing to some blouses in the shopping bag.

"You come with me," the man ordered, taking me by the arm. "You'll wait in my office while we call the police."

I tried to explain to the manager that I was just holding the bag for another girl who had given it to me outside the store. They didn't believe me. They claimed that I must have been in cahoots with Emmy. The police called my parents and told them that I had been caught with stolen merchandise. A saleslady recognized Emmy when the police brought her back to the store. The lady had seen Emmy at the counter from which the things had disappeared. Emmy denied having been there, but later admitted it when we were taken to juvenile detention. I got stuck with most of the blame because I was the one who had been carrying the stolen things. We were both put on probation. I remember my mother crying when she heard about it.

In high school I spent most of my time studying. The teachers thought I was smart because

I got mostly A's. But my good grades were really due to my lack of distraction from studying. I was glad to be at home reading or helping mother with her household chores. I guess I never was ambitious, except in my daydreams of being a famous artist or a well-known writer. Most of the time I think that I would be happiest if I were a wife, keeping house and taking care of children. But I doubt that I could take all that goes with it. I'm still a virgin.

Dr. Beatty helped me feel more relaxed than I was before I began therapy, but the relaxed feeling never lasted long after I left his office. He talked about my self-rejection and explained that my compulsions came from guilt feelings. He helped me most by assuring me that I was not losing my mind. He pointed out that being compulsive was a mental disorder, but that didn't make me insane.

I tried to do everything Dr. Beatty suggested. I rewarded myself with extra little treats when I was able to resist counting things over and over. I kept a chart of my progress in controlling myself when I felt the need to check the door repeatedly to see if it were locked. I took time out for deep breathing and imagining myself relaxing at the seashore listening to the waves. I did my best to remember everything Dr. Beatty said I should do in order to tie things that had happened to me in the past to my present behavior.

"I'm trying," I told him. "I'm trying to do what you suggest." Then something very powerful within me, which I couldn't control, made me repeat to myself silently, over and over again, "No, I'm not trying!"

I couldn't understand it. Why was I doing this? Why wasn't I cooperating? I went to Dr. Beatty to get his help. I was disappointed that in most ways I wasn't much better after all those weeks than I was when I had first come to see him.

I checked in late at work one day. To prevent this in the future, I made up my mind to get up an hour earlier on workdays. If we are late in reporting for work, management makes life miserable for us. Even if we are only a few minutes late, they cut a full hour from our vacation time. I was late because I spent too much time trying to make my bed the way mother would have made it. The fourth time I remade it, I almost succeeded. I was sure that if I had the time to make my bed just once more it would have looked the same as it would if mother had done it.

I was afraid that I wasn't responding to Dr. Beatty's therapy well enough to please him. I couldn't decide whether he really was disappointed in me or if I only imagined it. It scared me to think that my doubts would affect the outcome of my therapy. My headaches were beginning to come back. I agonized over whether my headaches came from my concern that Dr. Beatty might be disappointed in me if I shared my doubts with him. So I said nothing.

After a few more visits, Dr. Beatty told me he would refer me to another doctor for evaluation for medication.

"There is something new that has been proven helpful in reducing the symptoms of obsessive-compulsive disorders," he said. He made a phone call and got an appointment for me.

As I continued therapy over a period of several months, I began to feel more comfortable and less anxious about everything. Dr. Beatty told me that I had given up resisting. He said he wasn't sure whether it was the medicine or just the additional time we had spent together that was responsible for my improvement. At last I began to feel that I was shaking off a burden I had carried for most of my life.

It was eleven P.M. two months later. I was lying in bed reading. Now, reading just a page or two of a book was enough to put me to sleep. As I laid the book down on my night table, a fleeting question crossed my drowsy mind—Did I lock the door securely? The answer came to me clearly—Yes, I *know* I did!

At work the next day Mr. Sommers called

me into his office at the back of the store. He seemed upset.

"I don't know how much longer we can keep you here, Wilhelmina," he said as he sat down. "It might be best for you to look for another job. We can't put up much longer with the carelessness you've shown these past few months!"

## COMMENT:

*Wilhelmina found that, sometimes, "cures" have unexpected complications. Her boss could accept her as "peculiar" but not as "careless," as she seemed to be to him when she was no longer compulsive. He interpreted the change in her behavior as a loss of her previous zeal.*

*Obsessive-compulsive disorders usually begin in adolescence or early adulthood. They are equally frequent in men and women. They may range from moderate to severe. Wilhelmina's case was severe. Yielding to her compulsions became a major activity in her life. Compulsive disorders are accompanied by much anxiety and are likely to be found among people who have experienced excessive guilt. The guilt felt may not necessarily have a reasonable basis and might even be vicariously experienced. Obsessive-compulsive disorders tend to become chronic and are often difficult to treat without the use of medication as an adjunct to psychotherapy.*

*Recent studies suggest that mild forms of the disorder are much more common than had been previously recognized. In some professions where great* care must be taken to avoid errors, mild symptoms may be viewed as assets. When obsessions are present, there may be a phobic avoidance of specific people, places or situations on which the obsession is centered. A common example is an excessive fear of "germs" causing a person to avoid public rest rooms, shaking hands with strangers or touching door handles.

When Wilhelmina's symptoms disappeared, Mr. Sommers almost fired her. The reader may be glad to learn that, at her request, her therapist contacted him and explained the changes in her behavior. As a result, she did not lose her job. As time passed and she continued to be free of symptoms, Wilhelmina became a much more resourceful and valuable employee. After a year, she got a raise (without counting any item for which she was responsible four or five times).

*"The best thing for me to do is kill her right now!"
Walter decided. He was thinking about the woman
who wouldn't tell him where his mother was hidden.
He was sure it was somewhere in Viet Nam. Walter
is mentally ill, but can still straighten out fenders
and share a small rented house with his girlfriend,
Claire. He shouldn't have stopped taking his medication.*

# WALTER:
# Where Did They Hide Her?

My name is Walter. I found out that a woman
living four houses down from where we live
just came back from Viet Nam. What's strange
about that? She's not Vietnamese. She's white
and I'm guessing that she's got a good reason
for keeping what she did there to herself. Of
course, there were lots of white women in Viet
Nam during the war. But that was quite a while
ago. I have to find out what she was doing there
during the past few months. I don't care about
her good looks. It's important for me to know
what she was doing there and why she won't
talk about it.

I'm thirty-six and live with a woman ten years
older. Her name is Claire. She was out of a job

when the housecleaning company she worked for folded. I met her after I was discharged from the hospital. I found a job in the body and fender shop at MacKay's Buick. She was there looking for work as a cleaning lady at the car agency. After they told her there were no openings, she wandered over to our shop next door.

I was working outside on a dented fender. She walked right up to me and started admiring my work although it wasn't near finished. We hit it off right away and the next thing I knew we were living together in a small rented house on Egland Street. She wanted to live in a house because she said she was a homebody. It didn't bother her that I had been at the State Hospital. She said that she'd remind me to take those pills I'm supposed to take every day to keep me from thinking crazy thoughts. The pills make me jittery. I haven't taken any for a couple of months.

Body and fender work is good work. I like the guys there, but I don't socialize. They don't talk about anything I'm interested in. They talk sports and women and about always being short of cash. Some of the guys act like they're kind of scared of me. Once a guy asked me if anything was wrong because he saw me staring off into space at nothing at all. Well, nothing is wrong with me. I have my opinion of them and I know for sure I'd rather be me and have my thoughts than be one of them thinking all day about sports, women, and how broke they are. They all have to admit that I'm a good worker. The boss, Vic, gave me a raise two months ago. He knows that I don't fool around and don't spend time talking and joking. My thinking don't take no time from my work.

When Claire is busy, I do the shopping at the supermarket a couple of streets from where we live. Well, one time the lady who came from Viet Nam was standing behind me while I was waiting in the checkout line. I turned toward her very slowly, so as not to scare her or anything, and asked her how long ago she had left Saigon. She looked at me kinda funny and said that she'd never been there. She said I must have mixed her up with someone else. She said that the only place outside the USA she'd ever been was across the border in Mexico. I told her, "Sorry, lady. You just look like someone I saw in 'Nam when I was over there." But I knew that she had been there. She'd lied to me so I lied back to her. I wasn't ever in Viet Nam. When I tried to enlist, the Navy found out that I'd been at the State Hospital. I told myself that someday the lady would find out that I knew what she was up to.

I'm glad my having been in the hospital doesn't bother Claire. She said it won't bother her as long as I keep my good job so she can be a homebody. Besides, the psychiatrist and

those others who were in court on the day of
my discharge hearing said something about my
having a good chance to make it if . . . I
couldn't understand the words they used after
the "if."

This is another night I can't sleep. I kinda
half sleep and half dream. I am dreaming that
I'm pounding that lady from Viet Nam on the
head with the hammer I use for knocking out
dents in cars. I am screaming at her, "Tell me!
Tell me, you bitch!" The next thing I know,
Claire is shaking me. "You're knocking all the
guts out of that pillow," she says sleepylike,
but mad that I woke her. Then she sits up and
looks at me and asks, "Are you going crazy
again? Not in this house!" she warns, wagging
her finger at me. Then she turns over and goes
back to sleep. I wonder, does Claire know the
reason why the lady who lives down the street
is lying? I decide she does. How can I make
Claire tell me what the woman is hiding from
me?

I know I'll find out what their secret is if I
use my wits and take my time. This is hard
because I'm mostly impatient and want to know
things right away. Vic, my boss, knows the
reason that lady isn't telling anyone that she'd
been in Viet Nam. That makes three people. Or
four people? I don't know all the facts yet, but
I got a few good hunches.

It's easy to see that the lady from Viet Nam isn't aware that I am onto her game. She doesn't know that I think about her nights when I can't sleep, which is often. What I don't know is what she was doing there. There is a guy that's working with me named Karl. He knew what the lady was doing in Viet Nam. I asked him about it. I wasn't surprised that he pretended that he didn't know what I was talking about. He is always saying he's short of money. I wonder how much she is paying him to keep his mouth shut.

They say that my mother died in that car wreck in Ohio. No one except me knows the truth—that they kidnapped her and took her over to Viet Nam where my brother had died. That lady from down the street knows where they hid my mother. She knows where my mother is right now. One thing they can all be sure about is that I'm going to find out where they are keeping her. They probably paid that lady plenty not to tell anyone. She'll be surprised when I tell that I know all about it. She'll be even more surprised to learn that I know that it's not the Vietnamese who are keeping my mother there. It's the "others" who are keeping her a prisoner.

It's 5:45 A.M. My car is parked just out of sight of the lady's house. I don't mind waiting. I got all the time in the world. Yesterday when

Claire was out of the house I phoned the shop and told them I was sick. Last night I told Claire I had to go to work early this morning. Now I am sitting in my car parked where I can see the lady when she leaves her house. I'm just waiting and smoking and not thinking of anything. When, at last, I see the garage door opening, I say to myself, "This is it!" But a bald-headed guy in a small car backs out onto the driveway. As much as I can see of him in the early morning light, he's got a pasty face and a black moustache. I figure he must be her husband or her live-in. One brief look at him as he drives by is enough for me to know that he's the type I don't like. I never trust a guy with a pasty face and a moustache like his. Anyway, I know for a fact that she didn't tell him anything about Viet Nam. And I know the reason. She doesn't trust him any more than I do.

I take another look at the house. He left the garage door wide open. Quickly I get out of my car, run toward the house and creep into the garage. There's an old Chevy still parked in there. I shut the garage door behind me, hoping that the noise of its closing won't alert anybody. I jump into the back seat of the Chevy, bending low so that she won't spot me before she gets in. After I'm there I decide that if I'm in the car when she opens the door to the garage, she might spot me and I'll lose my chance. Quickly, I get out of the car and hide behind it.

It seems like just a minute after I get out of the car that the door from the house to the garage opens. There she is! I can see from her expression that she didn't expect the garage door to be closed. Pastyface probably leaves it open for her when he leaves in the morning. She shrugs and walks to the garage door to pull it up. It's something most women don't like to do. I'll bet she's planning to tell the guy off when he gets home. I notice that the lady is kinda too much dolled up for just working in an office. The people working with her don't know that she's employed by the ''others'' on the sly. ''Hey, stop!'' I tell myself, annoyed that I'm not thinking straight. The people in her office *are* the ''others'' themselves, hiding their real identity. Pretty shrewd! But they don't fool me. I can see through their disguises.

I think she hears me. I quickly step out from behind her car just as she is passing me to go open the garage door. I grab her and hold her tight so she can't move. There's a big scream. It sounds even louder in the small garage. If someone's in the house they sure could hear her. She starts shaking. Her eyeballs look like they might pop out. I tell myself her conscience is hurting her now that she's been caught.

''Where are you hiding my mother?'' I ask her calmly. I got her now, so there's no point in getting excited. I make my voice sound stern.

"You know where she is, so don't pretend!"
She is twisting, trying to bite my hand. I shove
the palm of my other hand into her face. She is
trying to say something. I let up a little on her
mouth.

"Yes, I've seen your mother," she says in a
muffled voice, her words coming out between
my fingers.

"Ah, you didn't get away with it, did you?"
I mock her.

"You win," she says hoarsely. "Let me go
and I'll tell you about it." I don't move. "Let
go of my arm and get your hand out of my
mouth," she croaks.

"First tell me where she is!" I demand.

"She's in a house," the lady says breathing
hard.

"Where?"

"In North Dakota."

"Liar!" I scream, grabbing her tighter and
pushing my palm against her face harder. "You
know damned well that she's in Viet Nam and
you came from there yourself six months ago.
I've kept my eye on you."

Suddenly, when I wasn't expecting it, she
gives a big heave and pulls herself away from
me. She starts running toward the door to the
house, but it had locked when she shut it. I went
after her.

"I didn't expect you to know that she's in Viet Nam," she said facing me and seeming much calmer now.

"I knew it all the time," I tell her.

"But I didn't take her there, so why are you mad at me?" she asks.

"I'm not mad at you. I just didn't want you to keep lying to me like you did at the supermarket."

She looks at me closely and I see a glimmer of recognition in her eyes. "Oh, yes, I remember you," she says. "You seem to be an OK guy—not the type that would hurt anybody." She kinda gives me a forced smile as she says it. "Let me fix you a cup of coffee and we'll call the guys who know exactly where your mother is," she says nodding her head like she's agreeing with me.

Now her voice becomes stern. "Get me the purse I dropped!" She points to it on the floor. "I need the keys to open the door." In a softer voice she asks, "Have you had breakfast yet?"

I think she won't tell me the truth. She is scheming to trap me. I wasn't born yesterday. I'm smart enough not to fall for her line. When she gets to a phone she'll call the "others" to help her get away from me. The best thing to do is to kill her right now—here in the garage with all the doors closed. It wouldn't be hard. She is small, but slippery, as I had found out.

"Let's go into the house. Maybe your mother is in there," she says softly, almost whispering.

"My mother is dead," I tell her and start to cry. "How can she be in the house? She died in a car crash in Ohio." Suddenly, I feel very tired. I glance up and see relief flooding over her face.

"What you need is a cup of good coffee," she continues. "I can make you the best cup of coffee you ever had in your life." She is pretending not to be afraid of me. But I know better. Her hands are trembling and her face is sheet white. I know she is trying to trap me. I was up all night last night. I just couldn't go to sleep. And now I am suddenly aware of how very, very tired I am.

I pick up her purse and hand it to her. She gets her keys out and opens the door. I follow her into the house. I watch her closely and see that she goes straight to the coffee pot, not to the phone.

The coffee is good. "It's what I needed," I tell her, trying not to listen to the voice inside me that says, "Kill her now!"

"Is it OK if I call my office and tell them that I'm going to be late?" she asks, giving me a smile that looks like she is trying to flirt with me.

"I know you're trying to trap me," I tell her

sadly. "You're trying to get me back into the hospital. I've fallen for all that stuff before." My voice is rising, "I don't want to go back there!"

When she doesn't say anything, it begins to dawn on me that the doctors and nurses at the hospital know where my mother is. But I don't want to go there to ask them where she is because I am afraid they'll keep me there.

"Who do I call to ask for your medicine?" she suddenly asks as she hands me a second cup of coffee and a muffin.

"Claire, the gal I live with," I tell her, and give her the number. Immediately, she goes to the phone and dials.

"Hi!" she says when Claire answers. "I've got. . . ." The lady looks at me, raising her eyebrows. "Walter," I tell her. "I've got Walter right here in my kitchen at. . . ." and she gives Claire her address. "He's sitting here at the table with me drinking coffee. He hasn't been feeling well and needs his medicine. He doesn't look like he's happy. Would you mind bringing over his medicine as soon as you can?"

I know she is tricking me. I know the police will be here soon to take me to the hospital. But now I'm ready to go. I'm sure that at the hospital they can help me find my mother better than this dumb dame could.

I hear the police. I am surprised at how fast they got here.

Note: I have invited Eva B. McCullars, M.D., a former colleague, now with Psychiatry Associates, Ltd., Yuma, Arizona, to write the comment for Walter's narrative. Dr. McCullars is a Diplomate, American Board of Psychiatry & Neurology.                    The author.

## COMMENT by Eva B. McCullars, M.D.:

*Paranoid schizophrenics usually have one or several systematized delusions related to a single theme. In Walter's case the theme appears to center on rejection by and distrust of women. Walter's history offers some clues, specifically, the premature abandonment by his mother who died in an automobile accident. His older brother was more acceptable because he didn't have mental problems and was eligible to join the military. He was later killed while serving in Vietnam. The boys' mother's ambivalence toward Walter could have preceded, or resulted from her preferred son's premature death.*

*Walter's mother's ambivalence caused him to question his competence as a male. Sexual identity problems remained with Walter throughout his relationship with women in general. Walter's mother loved him conditionally. She rejected him for not being able to measure up to his older brother but loved him as her son. Walter split his mother into a "good" accepting one and a "bad" rejecting one. The bad one he sent to Vietnam to get killed; the good one he accepted only in the presence of nurturing females.*

*Walter lived with a woman ten years older than himself who was a mother figure. Their relationship was most likely platonic. He was attracted to her when she offered him a nonthreatening caretaking relationship. Walter was threatened by his unwanted sexual feelings which were expressed in dreams of violence as when he dreamed of "hammering the lady on the head" while calling her a "bitch."*

*Walter's attraction to women conflicted with his fear of being unable to function adequately as a male and, therefore, be rejected by the lady "from Vietnam." Walter's delusional state resulted from his feeling of failure, his unresolved depression over his mother's death, and his inability to cope with his ambivalence. Walter saw serving in Vietnam as a symbol of courage that was inaccessible to him. It was a place where his brother was "man enough" to be sent and where he died honorably.*

*As Walter's stress increased, his unconscious material penetrated his conscious mind. When this happened it was more likely for his delusion to be acted out. Certainly, his failure to take his prescribed medication and the lack of professional supervision played a role. Because he was a failure in his mother's eyes, Walter hated her and tied this hate into predicate thinking, that is: Vietnam is death; mother is dead; therefore mother is in Vietnam.*

*Walter knew he was becoming ill under the stresses he was experiencing. He was attracted to the "lady" but he could accept her only if he could picture her as having been in Vietnam serving him as a potential caretaker and replacing his mother. As she denied having been there, he projected onto her the feelings he had toward his "bad" mother. However, when the lady participated in his delusional system, a chemical brain milieu of decreased threat occurred allowing him momentarily to lower his guard and acknowledge the truth.*

*Dr. Kent did not present Walter's narrative as a typical case of paranoid schizophrenia nor did he intend it to be used for making generalizations. However, there are characteristic signs of the illness in the narrative. The final outcome was lucky for the lady who so cleverly entertained her unwelcome guest.*

*Can someone who has split into two completely different personalities be unaware that they are really one person playing different roles? Can such a person live in separate worlds without knowing that this is happening? Surprisingly enough, the answer is "yes."*

*If you met Lisa in the following narrative, you wouldn't recognize Helen; and if you met Helen first, you would not imagine that a person like Lisa could inhabit the same body. It's no wonder that Mr. Huntington was confused when he tried to date Lisa. It was a pity, he thought, that Helen had to tag along and spoil everything.*

# LISA AND HELEN: Sisters Under the Skin

LISA: As soon as I arrived at our apartment I took the *Webster's New World Dictionary* off our small bookshelf and looked up "lascivious." I read the definition: "1. characterized by or expressing lust or lewdness; wanton. 2. tending to incite lustful desires." I got the idea, but just to be sure, I looked up "wanton." For "wanton" it said: "1. undisciplined. 2. sexually loose or unrestrained."

"Lascivious" means sexy. I don't know why those two guys at Neely's bar didn't just say that I'm sexy. They didn't look like college professors or guys who have fancy vocabularies. They wore old jeans, torn T-shirts, and their hands looked like they'd often been scrubbed with grease-dissolving soap. They weren't the type to use words like "lascivious." They couldn't have been showing off to me because they didn't know I was listening to their conversation. I shrugged. I guess I'll never figure out some men.

I don't need to hear that I'm sexy from those guys. I'm twenty-four and for more than ten of those years I've heard men say, "Lisa is sexy!" By now it's old stuff, but every time I hear it, it makes me feel good. I like to wear dresses that some people might call "suggestive." The necklines of the dresses I wear are cut low, and the skirts are above my knees. Men look at me and keep looking. I talk in a throaty voice that gets to them. I give them little hints that it's easy to turn me on. But they learn that my bait hasn't got a hook in it, when I insist on going home alone.

Of course, I can't pull that off every time. When I'm working at Lee's nightclub, I dance almost nude. Sometimes I get drunk after the show. Then I'm not sure what happens, but I've got a good idea. Right now I'd rather not think of that. I'd rather think of those two guys I overheard at the bar.

HELEN: It's not easy to keep our apartment looking neat and clean. My sister, Lisa, who shares the apartment with me is messy. I get annoyed that I have to spend so much time cleaning up after her. I've given up trying to be an example to her. Trying to keep her out of trouble is an unfair burden my family passed on to me when I left home. Lisa knows that I disapprove of her life-style, but I haven't been able to convince her to find an apartment of her own and move out. I can't force her to leave because I feel responsible for her. She fits the description I've heard of people one can't live with and can't live without.

At the office where I work, I wear tailored outfits that fit my wish to be conservative. Some of my coworkers think I'm a workaholic and say that I lack a sense of humor. I've even heard the words "prude" and "frigid," whispered more than once. Few people appreciate how hard it is for me to keep up appearances in spite of frequent headaches and feeling dead tired. I don't need to apologize to anyone for having high standards. I'm glad that I'm not lascivious like my sister Lisa is. The word "lascivious" slid into my thoughts out of the blue. I know what it means, although I can't recall hearing the word before, and I have no idea why it crossed my mind.

I've worked at Huntington and Keale Realty

for a year and three months now. Before that I lost some good jobs because of Lisa. She keeps barging into my life when I least expect her or want her to. I have warned her to stay away from me, but she refuses to listen. Whenever she interferes with what I am doing, something terrible happens. Once she turned up where I was working and tried to date my boss. She didn't know that the woman sitting at the desk in his office was his wife—not his secretary. Later, when I apologized for Lisa's behavior, my boss tried to date *me*! When he saw how shocked I was, he called me a hypocrite and fired me. The last thing he said to me before he slammed the door was, ''You need to see a psychiatrist!''

I have to cope with the constant fear that some day Lisa will show up where I am working now. That's why I try not to leave any hints in our apartment that could help her find out where the office is. Whenever she can, she tries to wreck my career. It's terribly unfair that people hold me responsible for what she does. But I guess everyone is judged, to some extent, by what their relatives do.

Last week Mr. Huntington asked me to step into his office. ''Helen,'' he said, ''your work is always accurate and finished on time. I want you to help me keep an eye on the file clerks and typists. When they don't know how to handle a problem, they waste time trying to decide what to do. I want them to ask you for help. You're more sensible than the others. Of course," he added, "that calls for a little raise." He mumbled the last sentence, lowering his head as if he were at confession.

One night I dreamed that I wanted to kill Lisa. In my dream, I tried to drown her by holding her head under the bath water while she was in the tub. I screamed at her, "I'm killing you because you are interfering in my life!" I kept repeating, "Stay out of my life! Stay out of my life!" In my dream, Lisa struggled as I tried to hold her down, yelling, "You bitch! You smug, superior bitch! You have always thought that you were better than me ever since we were kids! You're jealous of me because no guy ever tried to screw you. Even if they gave you a chance, you wouldn't know what to do!" In my dream I saw Lisa jump out of the tub and I heard her say mockingly, "Sorry, you won't get rid of me that easy, Sis!" Then she gave me a hard slap on the face. When I woke up, I felt like I had been beaten up.

LISA: At Lee's nightclub one evening, I planned to mow them down. It was late and I had to hurry so that I wouldn't miss the first show. I would be topless, as usual, but I had a real surprise planned for that crowd. I wanted to show them the real meaning of the word, "lascivious," without making them go to any dictionary!

I writhed in time with the music on the small stage. The leopard-skin G-string that covered my "no-no" part moved up and down with my motions. Suddenly my hand moved toward it as if I intended to pull it off. There was shouting, clapping, and the sound of stamping feet. As the uproar continued, I saw Mike, the manager, hurrying over toward me. As he passed me he whispered out of the corner of his mouth, "Don't do that again! See me in my office later." I finished my act as the crowd kept yelling, "Take it off! Take it off!"

When I stepped into his office, Mike was smoking his usual cigar and leaning back in his chair. As soon as he saw me he sat up, frowning. "Lisa, are you crazy?" he asked me, cocking his head to one side as if in disbelief. "Do you want the cops to close the place down? All it would take is for one of those guys out there to say we have nude dancing here." He looked at me as if he were studying me. "Lisa," he said slowly, "I think that there is something strange about you. You're trying too hard to prove something. I don't know what it is, but if you're not careful, you're going to get yourself and us into a mess of trouble."

HELEN: One evening, after I took my bath, I looked at myself in the mirror. There were deep shadows under my eyes. I was surprised that working at Huntington and Keale had caused them. It's the best job I ever had. I was determined to keep it even though it left me feeling tense and exhausted. I vowed that this time I wouldn't let Lisa make me lose it.

That night I couldn't fall asleep. I knew that Mr. Huntington had me in mind for a more important position. Maybe he'll ask me to become his private secretary.

I thought of my mother struggling to make ends meet with all of us children to support. Father spent his time out with the fellows drinking and chasing other women. My three brothers took after him, always teasing me, playing around, and getting into trouble.

Mom worked hard at two jobs so we could get by. She couldn't count on Dad. I respected her because, even with all of her responsibilities, she still took time out to teach Sunday school. Once, when Dad gave her a pat where no decent man would put his hand, I saw her face contort with disgust. My heart reached out to her in pity.

LISA: When I woke up I remembered that Helen had said it was my turn to go to the supermarket to buy the groceries this week. I had to drag myself out of bed. I didn't sleep well last night. I opened my eyes, stretched, and thought about making coffee. Years ago, at home, I used to bring Dad his first cup of coffee. I recall his smile when he saw me coming. He'd sniff the air and say, "You've brought me 'plasma.' Now I know I'll live." I knew that my dad liked me a lot. My brothers did, too. When I was only four years old, they started telling me that when I grew up I would make some fellow "very happy." Then, they'd look at each other and laugh. Of course, I didn't know what they meant until much later. While I was still a kid, I heard them boast that I could wiggle my rear in a sexy way. They made me prove it in front of their friend, who clapped and sang in time with my motions.

HELEN: At Huntington and Keale I was invited to attend a meeting in the conference room to discuss plans for opening another office farther uptown. I knew that only people who were important in the company had been invited to attend the meeting. I heard rumors that plans to promote me to a more responsible position would be discussed. I could feel my heart beat fast as I thought of my good luck.

Mr. Huntington, Mr. Keale, and the three other partners were present when I entered the mahogany-paneled room. They turned toward me and nodded in a friendly way. Suddenly, something seemed to snap within me. I found myself smiling.

"Helen," Mr. Huntington greeted me, "we have asked you to come. . . ."

I heard my voice become throaty. "My name is Lisa!" I said.

TWO WEEKS LATER

HELEN: When I caught sight of myself in a mirror, I became aware of how depressed I looked. I felt defeated that Lisa again lost me my job. Accepting myself as being worthwhile required that I have a job—any job—I thought, realizing how scarce jobs had become.

Nothing had ever given me the satisfaction that I got from working at Huntington and Keale. Now, I had serious concerns about my future and began to question whether I could cope with my anxiety.

While I was sitting around feeling sorry for myself one evening, I was surprised to get a call from Mr. Huntington. I had never expected to hear from him again.

"Helen," he said, "I apologize for the way I acted at the meeting. I had to do it for the sake of appearances. We've got someone to take your place here at the agency. She's doing a fine job, but. . . ." There was a pause. "I want you to come back to work for us starting tomorrow. I'll see to it that you get a promotion." He lowered his voice to a whisper. "My wife will be leaving town tomorrow to spend a week visiting her daughter."

## COMMENT:

*The onset of multiple personality disorder, also
called dissociative disorder, usually begins in childhood. As seen in the case of Lisa/Helen, the disorder consists of a person's splitting into two or more
separate personalities. These personalities may interact or remain isolated from each other.*

*The impairment in functioning and the ability to
hold a job by persons with dissociative disorders
depends on the kinds of roles the personalities
adopt, and the relationship they have with each
other. They may be friendly or distrustful or even
unaware that the other personalities exists. The personalities of Helen and Lisa were able to maintain
a relationship and interact by viewing each other as
sisters.*

*Lisa/Helen grew up in a dysfunctional family that
might have benefited from family therapy had the
parents been willing to obtain it. When a mother
shares her feelings of sexual rejection with her
daughter, the consequences are predictably adverse
to the daughter's later adjustment. Ongoing child
sexual harassment, as in Lisa's case, usually remains an unreported form of child abuse. It has
many elements in common with adult sexual harassment. Typically, when held accountable, the perpetrator insensitively excuses it as a joke.*

*A child is defenseless in such a situation as Lisa
was. She was not in a position to protest and, therefore, was forced to adapt to it with disruptive consequences in her adult life. The causes of dissociative
disorders are not confined to influences of parents'*

*conflicting sexual attitudes but, in general, represent a way of coping with incompatible personality-shaping attitudes influential in a child's immediate environment.*

*What did Helen do in response to the unexpected phone call from Mr. Huntington when he tried to date her? Did Lisa return to make that decision for her? She did not. Instead, Mr. Huntington's invitation brought the Lisa/Helen duality to a mental health clinic. In time, with therapy, the inner conflict that had split them was sufficiently resolved to enable Lisa and Helen to give up their separate identities and become one integrated person.*

*Dissociative disorders are found three to nine times more frequently in women than in men. The condition tends to become chronic and usually represents a difficult therapeutic challenge. Among methods that have been successful in treating this disorder are hypnotherapy, psychoanalysis, and behavioral therapy. In some cases, medication is used as a temporary adjunct to psychotherapy.*

*Travelers to wonderful, distant places often return home with exciting stories. But few adventures in this world can match the experiences of those who return from clinical death as Henry did—or did he? People sit up and take notice of those who return from beyond the edge of life. Strangely, those who have been "dead" may find that they left all of their former aches and pains behind them.*

# HENRY:
# Clinically Dead

My name is Henry. I left my office without completing my latest client's income tax. All day I had wanted to go to the library to look up my symptoms in the *Merk Manual*. When I got there, I took the manual from the library's reserve bookshelf, but found no listing under "stomach." Instead, there was a reference to "gastric, gastritis, gastrointestinal." Under "gastric" there was a listing of cancer, normal values, ulcer, anemia. I turned to page 735—cancer.

I read the paragraph on gastric cancer. As I had feared, most of my symptoms pointed to cancer. The manual said that X-ray studies, endoscopy, cytological studies, and gastric analysis were required to confirm the diagnosis.

Before I selected Dr. Wesson to be my doctor, I checked on his credentials. They were solid for internal medicine. I thought of the tests he had neglected to give me, and it occurred to me that what I really needed was a gastroenterologist. I could roll the name for "gut specialist" off my tongue as smoothly as any medical student. When I had first consulted Dr. Wesson a couple of years ago, I was impressed with him because he seemed thorough and took time to check me over carefully. He ordered upper and lower gastrointestinal x-rays. But gradually, Dr. Wesson seemed to be too busy with new patients, to pay much attention to me. The same thing happened when I consulted other doctors. After I saw them a number of times they seemed to pay less attention to me than they did at first.

That's why I had to depend on myself. I went regularly to the library reference room to look up my symptoms in medical books. Unfortunately, most of these books were printed five or more years ago, making them out-of-date. But I figured the descriptions of symptoms probably remained pretty much the same.

With increasing uneasiness, I read that my symptoms closely resembled those of stomach cancer: "heartburn, abdominal distention, heaviness in the upper abdomen, physical fatigue, rapid satiation at meals, sudden distaste for food (particularly meat)." As I read on, I realized why Dr. Wesson may not have recognized my cancer. One of the medical books explained, *"Often early signs of gastric carcinoma are attributed to other causes."* I continued reading, "After stools have become tarry and blood is vomited, the cancer is usually far advanced." It was frightening.

I saw myself again forced to make the rounds from Dr. Wesson to Dr. Weisbaum to Dr. Sutton to the walk-in clinic and, as before, back to Dr. Wesson with the new information I had gathered in my rounds. It was a no-win game!

The following day, on my way home from my office, I continued my medical research at the library. I read the description of a kind of stomach cancer called Zollinger-Ellison Disease. I was pretty sure that I didn't have it when I read that one of its prominent signs was diarrhea. Most of my life I've suffered from chronic constipation. I put the book down wondering why my wife, Ellen, kept telling me that I was a hypochondriac. Such people hear about a disease and are sure that they have it after reading its symptom. If I had been a hypochondriac, I would have thought I had Zollinger-Ellison disease, but I didn't. It's just that I didn't have the same faith in the medical profession that she did. I wasn't surprised to read that cancer signs are often attributed to other causes by doctors. If doctors had diagnosed my uncle's leukemia in time, he might still be alive today. I remember Uncle Dan as a great guy, too young to die! And I, too, am too young to die because of doctors' errors.

My thoughts turned to the task of locating another doctor. I dreaded having to sift through the list of gastroenterologists in the phone book. I had gone through that two years before when I was looking for a cardiologist. I never did find one capable of making sense out of my irregular pulse, loud heartbeats, and a blood pressure that kept going up and down like a yo-yo. I showed one cardiologist the records I keep of my blood pressure and pulse. He was not alarmed when he saw them. He told me I had nothing to worry about. But it seemed clear to me that the variations in my blood pressure couldn't possibly be normal. I went to see another cardiologist. He gave me some tests and told me to change my life-style. That didn't made a lot of sense to me. "Death and taxes are forever," it has been said. Well, there is job security in that! Doctors are in the death-prevention business and I am in the audit-prevention business. In a way, doctors are much better off, because dead people don't complain; audited people do. Glumly, I thought that if I ran my accounting business the way doctors run their medical businesses, I'd soon be without clients.

After I finished my library research, I drove

home. As I opened the door I heard my son, Rudy, warn Sandy, his sister, "Daddy is here! Be quiet! He's sick again!" Sandy is hyperactive and constantly talks in a high-pitched voice I find irritating. Rudy is twelve and Sandy is nine. By then they knew that their daddy needs to have it quiet in the house. Ellen greeted me with the usual, "How are you feeling today, Henry?" I doubted that my wife's question reflected genuine concern. She continued setting the table without asking me what I had found out at the library about stomach cancer.

As usual, I went right into the bedroom and took my temperature, 96.8—low! I took my blood pressure, 155 over 95—obviously too high! My pulse was speeding at 92 beats per minute. It was no better than it had been on and off for months. Certainly Dr. Wesson must know that this isn't normal! I recall how shocked I was when he suggested that I might want to see a psychiatrist. He seemed quite serious about it. I certainly wasn't going to see a psychiatrist! It was my body, not my mind, that gave me problems.

Ellen called me for dinner. I had no appetite. Nevertheless, to avoid an argument with her, I joined the family at the table. I ate slowly and chewed carefully. After dinner the children joined Ellen in the living room to watch a movie on TV. I stretched out on the reclining chair in the den, feeling bloated. The discomfort in my stomach felt like background music irritatingly out of tune. Ellen had served turkey hot dogs and beans. She knew that this kind of food was too spicy for me. Now I would belch all night long. I thought of my dwindling supply of Darvon—''benzodiazepam'' I called it when speaking to doctors. I wondered why Dr. Wesson kept hesitating to renew my prescriptions for tranquilizers. He was probably afraid I'd get addicted. But he should have known that there were times when I needed them to get a decent night's sleep.

Doctors weren't the only ones—a lot of other people didn't seem to take me seriously either. I didn't have many friends—perhaps because I wasn't interested in sports. Even though my clients listen to me with interest during tax season, I don't think they appreciate me. Sometimes I find myself daydreaming that I am standing in front of an audience of people who are listening to me with breathless interest. Ellen has had that opportunity. She has addressed her AAUW chapter twice. Once she talked on motherhood. If she is qualified to lecture on motherhood, why didn't she suggest that they ask me to speak on fatherhood? She knew how much I wanted to do that! I remember the time I was surprised that Ellen had given a talk on how to cope. I wondered why she got to talk on a subject on which she had no expertise. I felt I should have been the one to give that talk. I've done a lot of reading on shamans, witch doctors, voodoo, and of course, on various modern medical subjects.

I'm not hard to look at, dress appropriately, am friendly and consider myself intelligent. Why am I not well liked? It doesn't seem fair.

While feeling unhappy about myself, I remembered reading a magazine article describing what it's like to be dead. The article quoted people who had been declared clinically dead and returned to life because some remote thread failed to sever at the last moment. They reported entering a tunnel and seeing a bright flash of light just before they died. They recalled floating in space and looking down at their bodies. They said that they experienced an indescribable feeling of peace. I thought how beautiful it would be to die.

Suddenly, I started trembling and wasn't able to stop. I found myself sweating, and didn't know why. Was it from a fear of dying or from stomach cancer. Was my heart beginning to fail? I asked myself, "Shall I give up—just go ahead and let myself die?" It would be a release and bring peace. But I couldn't let myself do it. I was afraid I might not have the peaceful experience described by some of the people who had been at the brink of death.

The very next day, while I was driving home, a small car swerved out of its lane to avoid hitting a cyclist and struck my compact. Ellen rushed to the hospital where I had been taken and stayed with me until I regained consciousness. I had only a vague recollection of what had taken place. Ellen said that the police told her what had happened. I had been wearing my seat belt, but it had been too loose to prevent me from bruising my chest and hitting my head hard against something in the car. Ellen said that the doctor in the emergency room told her that I had a concussion, some torn ligaments, and irregular heartbeats. "Cardiac arrhythmia," I translated, feeling that she would like to know the proper medical term.

I told Ellen that I had a strange experience while I was unconscious. My heart must have stopped beating because I felt my life draining out of me. As I said this, I watched the monitor near my bed. It continued to record my heart rhythms that now seemed regular.

I told Ellen that I recalled hearing through a kind of haze the emergency-room doctor telling the nurse, "This fellow is clinically dead." I seemed to float through a tunnel. A few moments later, a burst of brilliant light, edged with all the colors of the rainbow, surrounded me. I saw my spirit rising from my body as it was stretched out on the gurney. I recall forgiving all those who had ever hurt me. As my spirit floated above my body, I experienced a deep peace.

Ellen looked doubtful. "Don't you believe me?" I asked, annoyed.

"It must have been a dream, Dear," she said soothingly.

I shook my head. I told her that I had described dying to Dr. Wesson when he had come to see me. The emergency-room doctor had told him that I had had cardiac arrhythmia after the accident. Dr. Wesson seemed interested in hearing how it felt to be clinically dead. He wouldn't have been interested if it had only been a dream.

"Did he confirm your clinical death?" Ellen asked.

"Of course! He knew it from my lack of a pulse, my failure to breathe, from the coldness of my body, absence of reflexes, and from seeing the flat line on the monitor."

Ellen seemed awed. "What an extraordinary experience that must have been! Thank God you came back to us," she said and kissed my forehead.

I knew that hospitals no longer keep patients as long as they used to, but the day of my discharge came faster than I expected. When I looked around my hospital room I saw flowers everywhere. Get-well cards were piled high on my bed table. I could hardly believe that so many people had sent flowers and written letters telling me of their interest in my having returned from the dead. Ellen told our neighbors about my experience, and our son overheard her. He described how I had been clinically dead to his teacher who told the class about it. Ellen said that the kids in Rudy's class envied him for having such a remarkable dad—one who had been dead and returned home. Somehow, the news even got to the newspapers.

How about in Sandy's class, I wondered. "Did the kids in her school hear about what had happened to me yet?" I asked Ellen.

ELLEN: Six months have passed since Henry was discharged from the hospital. He has been spending his spare time preparing talks on what it's like to be clinically dead. He now seems like an entirely different person. He is excited about a letter he received from a publisher sounding him out about writing a chapter in a book on returning from death. Henry no longer broods over his various former illnesses. I can't help worrying about some of the reckless things he does now. He is getting quite a potbelly, and his discovery of junk foods has me concerned that he's raising his cholesterol sky-high! When I talk to him about it he calls me a "worry bird.'' One would think he was a teenager the way he stuffs himself.

I must admit that something bothers me. In the hospital Dr. Wesson confided to me that Henry had never been even near death. He said that his irregular heartbeats hadn't been danger-ous, let alone life-threatening.

''Then Henry wasn't really clinically dead?'' I had asked, astounded. ''No more than you or I ever were,'' Dr. Wesson replied. ''It was Henry himself, not I, who decided that he had been clinically dead. I never mentioned that to him. The whole scenario is a product of Henry's own imagination. Interesting, eh?'' he said, looking devilish.

I guess Dr. Wesson read my thoughts and concerns. ''If you ever decide to tell him the truth, consult a mental health specialist before you do it,'' he advised. ''I can give you the names of several good psychiatrists. Henry is a nice guy but I'm glad that, lately, he has no need to see me. I'd just as soon not have him make my office his second home again!''

Something close to disgust came over me when I thought about Henry's recent public speeches describing his clinical death. It is wrong for him to be giving talks on something that never happened. So far, he has addressed several fraternal organizations, the local college faculty club, the American Society of Psychic

Phenomena, Rudy's Boy Scout troop, and—I couldn't repress a shudder—my own AAUW chapter!

As I tried to fend off Henry's new, vigorous sexual advances, I thought of how much easier it had been to love a hypochondriac than a faker who misleads people to gain self-importance.

Article in Recent *Science News*.

Recent research has shown that patients who were not in danger of dying but believed they had been, may experience almost identical out of body experiences, bright lights and great peace, as those who recovered after actually having been pronounced clinically dead by their physicians. Researchers have received a grant to give this unexpected phenomenon further study.

## COMMENT:

*Henry's fear of having stomach cancer and heart disease before his "clinical death" was a somatization of his inner conflicts, anxieties, and needs. Typically, Henry had no insight into his situation and refused to consider that the origins of his physical symptoms might have been psychological.*

*Patients who imagine or misinterpret symptoms tend to go "doctor shopping." This usually leads to a deterioration of a doctor-patient relationship.*

*Henry's obsessive health concerns affected his social and family life. His preoccupation with his imagined illnesses served to distract him from his poor self-image and inability to win acceptance from people in his environment. Hypochondriasis may occur among people within a wide range of intellectual and economic levels. Professional people like Henry are not exceptions.*

*The onset of hypochondriasis most commonly occurs between the ages of twenty and thirty. It is found with equal frequency among men and women. Its course is usually chronic. However, any significant event in a hypochondriac's life may dramatically alter the way the underlying anxiety is expressed. The instant notoriety and self-importance Henry gained from having been "clinically dead" met some of his needs, but failed to resolve his underlying conflicts. Therefore, we may predict that his euphoria is likely to be short-lived.*

*Ellen would certainly be able to tell you the different ways Henry expressed his conflicts, anxieties, and needs after his new-found popularity. One thing, regretfully, that she did not know, was that according to some research, comatose patients who fear death but were not actually in danger of dying, may experience a similitude to "clinical death" without "faking."*

*Gladys didn't know how many nights she stared at the ceiling instead of sleeping. Gradually, a feeling of unworthiness began to push everything else out of her mind. She no longer looked for a job. "Who would hire a person like me?" she asked herself. One day her mother put her arm around her and told her, "I have made an appointment for you to see a doctor. She is a psychiatrist. . . ."*

*But there was more to her recovery than psychotherapy. Help sometimes comes from a most unexpected source.*

# GLADYS:
# Unemployed in Glenville, Texas

I looked at the check made out to me for one thousand dollars, and fought the impulse to rip it into little pieces. I might have done so if the loss of my job hadn't made it so hard for me to keep contributing to the support of my parents. My unemployment compensation didn't stretch far, even in a relatively low-cost area like Glenville, Texas.

I read the letter again. "We are pleased to send you the enclosed check for one thousand dollars. It is in addition to your severance pay and final salary, which you received earlier. We are doing this because we appreciate your seven years of outstanding service to the Seasport Swimwear Company. You motivated the employees under your supervision to increase their work output to a high level of production. You accomplished this by encouraging the workers, making yourself available to them when they needed you, and taking a personal interest in them and their families.''

I felt my stomach turn as I read on. ''It was a proud moment for the Seasport Swimwear Company when, last year, the *National Manufacturer's Monthly Magazine* featured a short story about the success you achieved in raising our employee morale. We remain grateful to you as we reluctantly leave your friendly city to continue our operations in an area where the available resources will permit us to become more competitive.''

''Probably overseas where they can get cheap labor!'' I hissed between my teeth as I crushed the letter and threw it into the wastebasket.

The thought of having lost my job and the security I had counted on sent a wave of anger through me that left me wanting to cry as it receded. I realized that with only unemployment insurance as income, I was lucky to be living in my parents' home instead of in an apartment where I would have had to pay rent. Living at home with them was convenient for me since my parents depended on me for help with some of their chores. Also, the rent money I contribute enables them to enjoy a few extra luxuries. The part of the house where my room had been when I was a girl had been remodeled into a studio apartment to make living at home convenient for me.

Now, unemployed at the age of thirty-two, I wondered what life had in store for me. For the first time I thought that perhaps I should have gotten married like most of the girls in my high school class. However, in our town, the choice of men to marry was limited. In Glenville, people were old-fashioned enough to expect married women to be mothers and housekeepers, even if they held jobs. I didn't see myself as the housekeeping type and preferred to make my mark in the world of employment. Maybe it was the insecurity that's been with me since childhood that made me prefer remaining at home with my parents to playing the seemingly hazardous game of catching a husband. I never felt the need for the active social life that appeals to many single women.

After Seasport moved out of town, I was sure that I could get work at the large spinning mill, the other big source of employment in our town. Working at the "ole mill," as Glenville folk affectionately call it, was a tradition for generations of local people. The mill had been in operation since the Civil War and was intimately

tied to Glenville's lore. No one could have con-
ceived of Glenville without it.

My family had always been proud of my
grandfather's working at the "ole mill." He
had risen to a senior management position after
starting at the bottom as a loom spinner. My
dad had also been employed at the mill after he
graduated from high school. Later, he left the
mill to try his hand at a number of other jobs
elsewhere. But eventually he returned to the
mill to finish out his working years. I knew
some of the people in management there
through my dad and grandfather. I had preferred
to work at Seasport because I wanted to prove
to myself that I could stand on my own feet
without relying on "connections." Now that I
needed a job, I was glad to push pride aside. I
was grateful that I had connections at the mill
that could help me obtain employment there. I
was willing to start at the bottom because I
didn't doubt that, in time, I would again work
my way up to a supervisor's position. With my
connections and excellent references I was rea-
sonably sure that I would soon be working at
the "ole mill."

A middle-aged lady who headed the personnel department at the mill looked over my application and then promptly called Hank Willis,
the mill's current vice president of operations.
I knew that Hank had worked with my father

and my grandfather. Through the intercom I heard him say that he wanted to see me in his office. Getting this special treatment gave me a feeling of solid comfort. I was determined to show the mill people that no matter in what capacity they employed me, I would be a worthy representative of my dad's and grandfather's reputations. While walking to Hank's office I passed some of the mill's employees in the hall. Seeing them gave me a ''family feeling'' that I had never had at Seasport.

Hank Willis welcomed me courteously. I felt reassured as I sat down in the chair across from him. He was as tall and lanky as my grandfather had been, and like many senior officers at the mill, was a native son. He remained quiet and subdued after I was seated. He seemed to be thinking of what to say.

After several minutes he started reminiscing about the ''old days'' at the mill. He told me that my grandfather had been greatly respected by both the workers and management. He added that my grandfather had increased the efficiency and morale of the employees by listening to their grievances and being willing to make changes to improve working conditions. It sounded very familiar. They had said the same thing about me at Seasport. He went on about how the mill had been modernized and enlarged while my father worked there. It was at the time when we were at war. The mill had to increase its output to meet the needs of the military services.

I wondered when Hank would get to the subject of my application. I thought that maybe he felt obliged to have a social visit before getting down to the details of my employment. At last he said, speaking slowly, "In view of your father's and grandfather's careers here and your excellent work at Seasport, I'm sure you know that we'd very much like to hire you, Gladys. I don't doubt that you would become a valuable employee if we had an opening here for you at the mill." He hesitated. "But there is a good reason why we can't offer you employment. We're broke!"

Realizing that I was not understanding what he was telling me he explained, "Foreign manufacturers are underselling us in everything we make." He continued, "There's no way we can compete with them. It's just a matter of time before we'll be out of business." His shrug suggested resignation.

Hastily I thanked him, said good-bye and left without meeting his eyes. I didn't want him to see the hopelessness I felt at hearing what was going to happen to the "ole mill." I had been so sure that I would find employment there that I had made all kinds of plans on how I would spend the money I thought I soon would be earning. My interview with Hank seemed like a bad dream. It reminded me of the nightmares I used to have when I was a child. The insecurities that I thought I had mastered years ago, now returned full force and, with them, came the fear that I was unworthy of being employed. I was sure that I would never find employment again. In the weeks that followed, I even began to believe that I had been fired by Seasport because I had done something wrong. They probably just didn't tell me what it was because they wanted to spare my feelings.

That evening, and in the days that followed, I was hardly able to stand the sight of food. My mother began to worry about my lack of appetite, and refused to accept my explanation that I was dieting. She insisted that I wasn't fat and didn't need to diet. Mother likes to fuss over me even though I'm no longer her little girl. I was glad she didn't know how many nights I stared at the ceiling instead of sleeping. Gradually, the feeling of unworthiness began to push everything else out of my mind. I started to believe that my sleeplessness was punishment for not having done the right thing with my life. It had been wrong of me not to get married and raise a family. Now I was destined to suffer the consequences of my mistakes. I spent most of my remaining energy trying to hide my true feelings from my parents.

I no longer bothered to look for a job. After all, who would hire a person like me? My mirror told me that I was far from attractive. Finally it seemed to me that my mind wasn't functioning right. I couldn't even concentrate on the morning newspaper. I couldn't answer letters from friends. I kept misplacing my keys and glasses and even a pair of shoes. At times, I wished I were dead and, after a while, this wish began to dominate all of my thinking. I thought about killing myself, but I didn't know how to do it. Besides, I didn't have the energy necessary to go through with it.

One evening my mother came into my room and found me crying. She put her arm around me and said, "Baby, I have made an appointment for you to see a doctor. She is a psychiatrist." My mother stroked my hair. "Dad and I are sorry we waited so long before calling a doctor, but we were afraid that you would be angry with us if we interfered. You always told us not to be so concerned about you because you wanted us to treat you like an adult. But we love you and are very worried about you." I leaned against my mother and cried. "Have I ever been an adult?" I asked myself. Mother kissed me and said softly, "My poor baby. My poor baby." Dad came in, put his arm around me and said gently, "Gladys, we love you, Honey."

The next day my parents drove me to see the doctor. When I was seated in her office, I didn't even look at her, much less answer her questions. Even though I sat across from her, she seemed very far away. I told myself that she was a stranger who I did not want to know. The doctor spoke to my parents after my visit and suggested that I start taking some medication that she prescribed. The one thing I remember real well is the relief I saw on my parents' faces as we left the doctor's office. Her receptionist handed me a schedule of appointments for the next several weeks.

As the weeks and months went by I realized that I was beginning to take more interest in life and had fewer and fewer wishes of wanting to die. My parents watched me carefully while I continued in therapy. I could feel their elation as my appetite improved and, in many ways, I seemed to become my old self again. However, I could not overcome the hopeless feeling that I would remain unemployed for the rest of my life.

One day shortly after I had begun to feel better, I was invited to attend the meetings of a group of former employees of the Seasport Swim Company. I was glad to join them. They said that their purpose was to get even with foreigners whose cheap labor had been responsible for the loss of our jobs. In time, former employees of the "ole mill" who had been laid off also joined our group. These days the mill was barely kept going with a skeleton staff. Several people whose business had failed because of the closing of Seasport and the slowdown at the mill also began to attend our meetings. We started the meetings with the Pledge of Allegiance to the flag. We felt we were patriotic because we wanted to save the United States from financial ruin because of cheap foreign labor. We tried to contact other groups throughout the country who wanted to rid the United States of foreign commercial influences. Some in our group suggested we have bumper stickers printed, reading, "America is for Americans!"

Unemployment continued to grow in Glenville. Some members of our group who were pretty bitter because they had lost their jobs at the mill even suggested that we create an incident that would give our cause visibility. At first I didn't like the idea. Then I kept thinking about the loss of my job and self-respect. After a while I agreed that this might be something to consider, and I was assigned to a committee to explore ways to dramatize the fact that foreigners were causing us to lose our jobs and we were not going to put up with it any longer.

My involvement with this group seemed to be good for me, probably because it gave me a direction in life. My feelings of well-being increased even more after I became the editor of the group's new newsletter. My parents were delighted to see that I no longer seemed depressed and that my appetite again was what it used to be. The only thing that had not fully returned was my self-confidence. To regain that, I thought that I would need employment where I could get the kind of approval I used to get at Seasport. I realized that the employees I supervised there had become a substitute for a family of my own. I missed caring for them and keeping them contented at their work. The activities of the group I was involved with now somehow failed to provide me with these same satisfactions. As time went on it seemed that my depression was returning.

After a few weeks I found myself sitting on my bed fighting to keep my tears from flowing. I hoped that Mother wouldn't come into my room one of these times and find me crying. I thought about returning to the psychiatrist for more medication and therapy, but decided against it. No matter what medication she could prescribe, it wouldn't bring me the job I needed in order to be satisfied with my life. At night I kept dreaming that we had declared war on several foreign nations. In the morning I would regret that it had only been a dream.

After one particularly restless night, I went

to the front door, still half-asleep, in response to the doorbell. It was the mailman with a registered airmail letter addressed to me from a company with a strange name. The return address didn't make sense to me. I opened the letter and read:

"We have decided to build our second U.S. electronic assembly plant in Glenville, Texas because of the pool of available skilled workers there. We assume that a large Japanese venture would be welcomed." I continued reading with disbelief. "We have a great interest in having you join our company. We read, in last year's 'National Manufacturer's Monthly Magazine' about the innovative employee supervision methods you introduced when you were employed at Seasport Swimwear Company. Your approach to management-employee relationships seems compatible with our philosophy of personnel management. We hope that you will seriously consider employment in our corporation and accept our invitation to visit Japan at our expense to become familiar with our policies and the products we manufacture.

"After your orientation and a brief training period in our methods of manufacturing we would hope that you would return to Glenville as an important member of our team and, of course, you would earn. . . ."

I stopped, and started reading the letter again from the beginning.

## COMMENT:

*Employment at Seasport Swimwear had given Gladys financial independence and enabled her to utilize her talents for working creatively with the employees she supervised. At the time, she had few friends outside of work. She was unable to absorb the loss of self-esteem and financial security caused by the loss of her job. She suffered a second blow when she failed to obtain a position at the "ole mill" where she had been certain her family connection would enable her to find employment.*

*Gladys could not tolerate the loss of self-esteem caused by these two events. She succumbed to a serious mood disorder called Major Depression, Single Episode. This may occur with or without delusions. Among the common symptoms are a depressed mood, diminished interest in activities, lack of appetite with a weight loss, inability to sleep, or sometimes, too much sleeping. Other symptoms of a major depression may be inability to concentrate, preoccupation with one's worthlessness, and thoughts of suicide. Dissatisfaction with herself caused Gladys to have a recurrence of these symptoms, as do about fifty percent of persons with the diagnosis.*

*After she had therapy, Gladys drifted into a situation that satisfied her need to interact with people. Unemployment and economic stagnation created a fertile soil for resentment.*

*What did Gladys do after she received the unex-
pected invitation to work for a Japanese company?
She accepted the job without too much soul search-
ing. After her training in Japan, she was employed
as a supervisor at the new electronic assembly
plant.*

*In time, Gladys had friends both in town and at
work. She found growing bonsai trees a fascinating
hobby.*

*Anne's mental deterioration caused by Alzheimer's disease was gradual and devastating. Was it inheritable? her daughter, Joan, wondered. She pictured herself sitting in a wheelchair like her mother, a victim of Alzheimer's disease. She thought of plaques and neural tangles in her brain and shuddered. Mrs. Tuttle, her social worker, helped her cope with her fears up to a point. Unsuspected by both—worse things than mere fears were to come.*

# MOM AND JOAN:
# In Separate Worlds

Excerpts from Anne's Letters.

December, 1987

Dear Marjorie,

It means a lot to me to keep in touch with you all these years since we graduated from high school and you moved East. Now, Christmas is almost here and, can you believe it, I nearly forgot to write my yearly update letter.

I didn't visit Bobby, Clara, and my grandchildren this year. I didn't feel up to traveling that far. Nowadays, I seem to forget where I put my glasses, my keys, and even the letters I bring in from the mailbox.

I'm over sixty years old and I guess the time

has come for me to pay the cost of aging with the coin of memory loss. The price is fair. Lost things turn up after a while, and I continue to enjoy life. Have a good holiday.

Love,
Anne

December 1988

Dear Marjorie,

Another year has gone. I hope all is well with you. Did I write you that they wouldn't renew my driver's license? Joan now has to drive me to the stores and doctors. She's a loan officer at the bank and does it between appointments. It's not as if I were taking her away from her family. Joan didn't remarry after her divorce and there were no children.

Merry Xmas. Remember me to your husband. His name is Richard, isn't it? I never was good at remembering names.

Love,
Anne

December 1989

Dear Marjorie,

Joan reminded me that tomorrow is Christmas. I feel sorry for her. She was so lonely that she made me move into her apartment with her. She took me to have tests of all kinds because she thinks there is something wrong with me. I can't get around anymore without her. Things are not so good for me now.

Love,
Anne

December 1990

Dear Marjorie,

Sorry about the poor handwriting. I've had a terrible year. I'm sending this from the hotel where I live now. Joan moved me to this place a few months ago. A lot of people in wheelchairs and some dressed in white clothes live here. Can you help me get out of this place and move in with you?

Love,
Anne

Dear Mrs. Johnson,

I visited my mother at the nursing home this afternoon. She has Alzheimer's disease. A lot of my mother's memory is gone. Sometimes she thinks that she is still in high school with you. Just keep sending the postcards. She enjoys them and she still knows who you are. I pin them on her bulletin board with the pictures of Bobby, Clara, and the grandchildren. You are a loyal friend.

Sincerely,
Joan

I had come to visit my mother in the nursing home. When I saw the old woman with the stained teeth and empty eyes sitting in her wheelchair, I asked myself, ''Is this really my mother?'' As usual, she was lined up with a group of other residents along a wall near the nurses' station. Why didn't they clean her teeth, I wondered as I approached her. They were supposed to give her personal care. I was angry, but never made a fuss. I was afraid that if I complained they might, in some way, take it out on Mom when I wasn't around.

''Mom,'' I said, ''I'm Joan. I've come to see you.'' Slowly, her head moved in my direction, but her expression didn't change. I wheeled Mom into the room she shared with three other residents. Fortunately, they were usually quiet and didn't interfere when I visited Mom.

I had brought along a small photo album and showed her a picture of my brother and his wife, Clara, sitting together on a sofa. Clara was holding a baby on her lap.

''Now there is your son, Robert,'' I said, pointing. ''There is his wife with your grandson, Bobby! They're living in Pennsylvania and we are in California.''

My mother's eyesight had not been destroyed by her illness. A ghost of a smile appeared on her face as she seemed to recognize her son, her daughter-in-law, and her grandson. It was startling to see the tiny, thin smile accompanying the flicker of recognition. For a brief moment it changed her total appearance —unfortunately, always just for a moment. Most of the time, when I visited her, I held her hand and we sat silently together in the visitors' lounge—each in our separate world.

Who knows what her world was like? I often wondered when I sat with her. Was it more peaceful or more troubled than my own? Visiting Mom gave me time to think about my world and about our lives before her illness.

Mom had always been outgoing before she became ill, and I was reserved and inward looking. I could recall how attractive and popular she had been only six years ago before she gradually began to lose her memory. By today's standards she wasn't very old—barely over seventy. Alzheimer's disease had done this terrible thing to her. It seemed incredible!

After returning home from visiting Mom, the sounds and sights at the nursing home were sometimes replayed in my mind at night and kept me from sleeping. I had read articles in newspapers that Alzheimer's disease tended to run in families. It worried me to think that I might end up with it when I got older. In my mind, I could see myself sitting in a wheelchair in a nursing home, alone, with no one to visit me. I'd much rather be dead.

With time, my fears of ending up like Mom increased and started to interfere with my work at the bank. It was then that I decided I had to try to get professional help. I had heard some good things about a Mrs. Tuttle, a social worker, from others who had loved ones in a nursing home. Her practice, I was told, consisted of counseling family members with relatives suffering from serious illnesses.

I was tense when I walked into the counselor's office for my first appointment. I relaxed a little when I found myself in a pleasant, home-like room. A vase of yellow flowers stood on the desk and pastoral landscapes were on the walls. As I entered, Mrs. Tuttle rose to greet me with a smile. No one could have looked less like what I had expected. She was a middle-aged woman, stout and red-faced. She wore a loose, pink and red checkered dress. There was a comfortable dishevelment about her, which I found disarming. I began to feel at ease as I reclined in the well-padded chair in her office. By the time she asked me what she could do to help me, I had relaxed.

"My mother has Alzheimer's disease and I am having a hard time because I am afraid I have the same fate in store for me," I said, sighing.

"It's not unusual to have such fears," Mrs. Tuttle told me. "There are studies suggesting that certain proteins, perhaps genetic in origin, may play a role in Alzheimer's. But it is not inherited in the sense that you think. There are many factors and unknowns in Alzheimer's disease. You really have little basis for thinking that you will get it just because your mother has it.'' Mrs. Tuttle looked at me carefully to see how I was taking what she had said. "Besides, the methods of diagnosis and even the treatment is getting better all the time,'' she added.

I wasn't totally reassured. I thought that Mrs. Tuttle might be too good-natured to tell me something frightening, even if it were true.

"Sometimes unwanted thoughts come into my mind. I have found it useless to try to control them. Mostly, they have been about wishing that Mom were dead.'' It was hard for me to hold back my tears.

"That is not uncommon nor unexpected,'' Mrs. Tuttle said in a gentle, reassuring voice.

"If I wished for her death only for her benefit it would be easier to accept,'' I told her, looking down. "I wish her to die for my own convenience,'' I blurted out.

It was amazing to feel another facet of my personality emerging as I talked. Anger now was rising within me, replacing my previous feelings of guilt. "It isn't easy for me to drive to the nursing home three or four times each week. It is depressing to sit with an empty shell of a human being and wonder—is this all that really remains of my mother?''

''It's natural for you to have both guilt and anger under these circumstances, Joan.'' Mrs. Tuttle seemed really to be a gentle person.

I shook my head. I couldn't agree with her.

''Sometimes, as I sit next to my mother holding her hand, I feel myself actually hating her. She ruined my life!'' I said with my voice rising.

A slight upward movement of the counselor's head may have denoted surprise, but she remained silent.

''Sometimes when I sit beside her, I think of my dad,'' I continued. ''He died when I was in my early teens. I remember that Mom always used to nag him, and it made me feel sorry for him. After Dad's death, Mom had to be both father and mother to my brother, Robert, and me. I always felt that Mom liked my brother better than me and gave him privileges I never got. I used to resent her limiting my dating when I was in high school. My brother could date any girl he wanted.''

Mrs. Tuttle said, ''Can you tell me more about why you feel that your mother didn't love you?''

''Whenever I began to get serious about a

man, Mom would disapprove of him. The guy I actually married, Harry, was the one exception. He was wily enough to have played up to Mom. He did it with such obvious hypocrisy that I marvelled at how she could have been taken in by him. Although I was attracted to Harry, I didn't love him. I married him mostly to please Mom. I divorced him a year later." I felt my throat tightening.

"I understand," Mrs. Tuttle said quietly. I thought that she was too good a person to really understand. I wondered whether I should ever have come to consult her.

"What else can you tell me about your feelings toward your mother?"

I had said it all and it hadn't seemed to have made much of a dent on Mrs. Tuttle's thick skin! As I sat now, much less relaxed than earlier, the picture of my old, shrivelled-up mother came back into my mind. As I thought of Mom, a curtain descended and was then raised. Now the scenario had changed. I no longer felt that I could blame Mother, but rather that I was the one who had been at fault. I didn't have to let her influence me in my choice of a husband. Marrying a person I couldn't love was my own mistake. It had made me miserable enough that I decided never to consider marrying again. The hands on the clock on the wall in Mrs. Tuttle's office moved several minutes before she spoke.

"Are you thinking now that, maybe, you have been too rough in placing all the blame on your mother?" I was surprised. How did she figure that out. Obviously she was more insightful than I had thought.

"Do you think that you might be having guilt feelings because you placed your mother in a nursing home?" Mrs. Tuttle's brown eyes met mine.

I could not reply.

"Are you in some way blaming yourself for your mother's Alzheimer's disease? Is it possible that your mother's old-fashioned upbringing clashed with your own generation's values? Could it be that what at the time seemed to you like nagging was really concern for your Dad's health? Could your feelings that your mother preferred your brother simply have been due to your own insecurity?" Her eyes never left my face.

"We don't really know, do we?" she continued. "It's hard to judge people in retrospect. But one thing we do know is that nothing distorts memory like guilt does. On the other hand, you might have been right about all or some of your thoughts about your mother. It's hard for you to judge her now."

When she finished, I felt a glimmer of truth I had never accepted before—I didn't hate Mom. I hated myself.

"I am going to ask you to contact the Alzheimer's Family Center," Mrs. Tuttle said. "They will refer you to an Alzheimer's support group in your neighborhood." She gave me a phone number and made another appointment for me to see her the following week. I felt some of the tension I had built up leaving me.

As I left her office I asked myself if I felt better for having consulted her. The answer came to me slowly. It was both "yes" and "no," but mostly "yes," I decided. I hadn't planned to learn as much about myself in the counseling sessions as I had.

The following day I phoned the Alzheimer's Family Center. "My mother has Alzheimer's disease and she's in a nursing home," I told the woman who answered. "My emotions are all mixed up. My counselor suggested that I call you."

"I'll be glad to give you the phone number of an Alzheimer's support group in your neighborhood. They get together to discuss their problems. Also, I shall send you literature that explains what we know about Alzheimer's disease."

"What is the Alzheimer's Family Center?" I asked her.

She replied, "It's a private organization that helps family members who have someone with

Alzheimer's disease living at home with them. They offer a day care program for patients.''

The thought struck me that maybe Mom could have lived at home with me longer if I had taken her to such a family center. I should have looked into this before I put her in the nursing home, I told myself. That's what I would have wanted if I had Alzheimer's disease.

I felt myself shuddering at the thought. It brought to mind what I had read about Alzheimer's disease: ''neural tangles,'' ''characteristic plaques,'' ''onset earlier than senile dementia.'' One book in the library called it the ''silent epidemic.'' It said that five percent of the American population over 65 had it. That amounted to more than 2 million people.

Before my next appointment with Mrs. Tuttle I got a call from a woman from the local Alzheimer's group. She told me that eight or so people met regularly to exchange ideas and share their feelings with each other. She invited me to join them. I felt relieved. By sharing my thoughts and problems with others, I hoped that I would, at last, get the relief from guilt that I couldn't deal with.

There were five women and two men in the group. In a very short time I felt comfortable and at home with them. How wonderful they were! Gratefully, I thought, here were people who would understand me. Life would be better for me soon, I hoped. But deep within me there was doubt. I felt that I didn't deserve to be happy.

Two days after that meeting, the head nurse from the nursing home phoned and told me that my mother had just died. She said that as Mom was dying she had called out, ''Joan! Joan!''

I felt angry at myself for not having been there when Mom needed me. I realized then that Mom and I had not lived in separate worlds after all. Her world was part of mine and without hers, my world collapsed. I found it impossible to think of what this meant to me. I phoned Mrs. Tuttle and told her of my mother's death. When she heard the news she made an immediate appointment.

Later that day I sat in Mrs. Tuttle's office, grateful to be there. Both of us were silent. Suddenly, the floodgates opened and my flowing tears were a torrent. Then, within me, as it had previously, a curtain seemed to descend and then was raised. I stopped crying. I felt a muscle in my face twitch and my hands become tight balls.

Gently, the counselor told me, ''I know how you feel, Joan. Is it possible that death is what your mother may have wished for herself, as we all might in her circumstances?'' She paused. ''When I lost my mother it was as hard for me as it is for you," she continued. "Right now you are overwhelmed by grief, Joan. It's natural because you loved her so much!"

"You are wrong!" I snarled. "I am crying because I hated her so much and still do!" I was amused at the startled expression on Mrs. Tuttle's face.

That's why I gave her Alzheimer's disease," I said, singing the words.

I watched the counselor, suspiciously, as she picked up the telephone receiver. Before I could stop her she had dialed a number.

## COMMENT:

*Joan succumbed to a Brief Reactive Psychosis in which there is a sudden onset of psychotic symptoms which may last from two hours to as long as a month. It may be accompanied by incoherence, bizarre behavior, suicidal or aggressive behavior, hallucinations or, as in Joan's case, delusions. It may occur in susceptible persons after a major stress such as the loss of a loved one or other severe trauma. It is usually preceded by emotional turmoil caused by overwhelming perplexity or confusion.*

*Would Joan have been able to avoid a mental breakdown if she had joined the Alzheimer's support group earlier? It is possible that she might have done so had she established a mutually supportive relationship with some of the members or the group earlier in the course of her mother's illness.*

It took Joan several weeks of hospitalization to recover sufficiently to be discharged. In time, with the aid of psychotherapy and group therapy, she was able to gain an acceptable self-image. Two months after her discharge from the hospital she went back to her former job.

With Alzheimer's and other diseases where there is progressive destruction of brain cells, there is ongoing research that looks promising. Even as I write, experiments with human nerve growth factors seem to keep alive damaged clusters of the cells necessary for memory. There are experiments involving genetically altered genes that some day can be transplanted into the brain to serve specific repair functions. At present we must wait, but for the future, there are signs of hope.

*When Bill told the guys at the shop that he was
going to be hypnotized, Doug warned him that some
people believed that hypnosis was the work of the
devil. At his first session, the psychologist tested
him to see whether he would be a successful candi-
date for hypnosis. He told Bill that he could not
open his eyes. Bill really tried, but simply couldn't
open them until the psychologist told him he could.
It was scary. No one would blame him for wanting
to cancel his next session. But he didn't. He showed
up and was hypnotized. As a result, he almost had
an experience too long denied him.*

# BILL:
# Successful Hypnosis?

The leather chair in the psychologist's office
looked roomy and comfortable. I sat on the first
three inches of the seat.

"We don't often have people come here just
to be hypnotized," the psychologist told me
after he finished reading the form I had filled
out.

He seemed to be annoyed by the way I had
answered the questions. The psychologist had a
good reputation, but I didn't think that I was
going to like him.

"Why do you want to be hypnotized, Bill?" he asked, looking at me as if he didn't like hypnotizing people. I wondered if maybe he had had a bad day.

"I'm depressed," I told him, feeling it. "I want to be happy like other people."

"You want me to hypnotize you so that you will be happy?"

I nodded. "I saw people hypnotized on the stage a couple of years ago. They were laughing so hard they couldn't stop." I paused, remembering. "I don't think I've laughed for years. I want to forget my troubles and be happy—even if just for a little while!" I looked at him to see if he showed pity. There was none.

"Let me tell you something," the psychologist said raising a finger. "In a way, hypnosis is like surgery. You open a person up psychologically when you hypnotize him. It doesn't belong on a stage anymore than an operation does. The lack of laws restricting the practice of hypnosis is terribly regrettable!"

I wondered why he was telling me this. I'm a patient. I'm not in the legislature. I began to think I might be wasting my time.

The psychologist leaned back and crossed his legs. Then he continued, "There are some people in the mental health profession who believe that hypnosis is a therapy in itself. I am not one of them." I was sure now that I had come to the wrong place for help. I didn't come to hear a lecture.

The psychologist's voice became more sympathetic. "Why do you want to be hypnotized?" he asked, observing me.

"Because I am depressed," I reminded him. I wanted tears to come to my eyes, but they didn't.

His shrewd eyes studied me.

"And why are you depressed?" There was more gentleness in his voice now.

"Family problems," I replied, sighing deeply. At age thirty I dreaded the questions I expected him to ask about my childhood. I felt sure he wouldn't take my side, even if I told him how unreasonable my parents had been when I was a child. He'd think it was my fault that I got into trouble at school for smoking and for not going along with the school's dress code. I didn't want to bring all that up now.

"I'm referring to my present family," I explained.

"Family problems?" It seemed almost as if he had expected that.

"Yes, my wife doesn't love me," I said hoping that he would catch the sadness in my voice. I thought of Laura, working at the employment agency, always complaining about our bills.

The unpleasant disagreements we were having rankled when I thought of what a good husband I had always been. I felt the familiar tightening in my chest.

"My wife doesn't know how important her love is to me, and she forgets how much I deserve it." The tears now welling up in me were genuine.

I waited in vain for the psychologist to respond. Had he been paying attention to what I was saying?

"And that's why I'm depressed!" I continued, my voice rising.

"You are employed as an appliance repairman at A-1 Appliance Repair Company?" the psychologist asked, consulting the information sheet again.

"Yes," I replied, annoyed that he was changing the subject.

"And you have worked there for four months?"

I nodded, wondering what that had to do with hypnosis.

"And how do you get along at your job?"

"Great" I lied. I expected him to try to pin my family problems on job dissatisfaction. "It's a good place to work," I added, hoping to avoid what I thought might be a trap.

I tensed as the shrink looked at me. Did he

know that I was lying about getting along at my job? For a moment I considered telling him about my bad luck in always winding up in jobs where the bosses are turkeys, but I decided it would be safer to change the subject.

"I have a bum back and frequent head-aches," I told him, anticipating his next question. "My wife is taking medicine for high blood pressure. My daughter is seven and gets speech therapy. Except for that, we're all in good enough health." I looked at the man sitting across from me. I failed to see in his eyes the compassion that I thought should be there if he were a good psychologist.

"You believe that no one loves you?" he probed.

"Yes, I do feel that," I admitted, certain that our conversation was going nowhere. In spite of my frustration, I found myself reclining comfortably in the big leather chair.

"How about relatives, friends, veteran buddies—none of them love you?"

"No, not really," I replied after thinking it over. "I have an older brother in the navy. I haven't heard from him for years. My uncles, aunts, and cousins live across the country and never visit."

"Family problems can be rough," the shrink said in what seemed an offhand manner.

"I could get drunk!" I suggested, becoming impatient. "But my dad died of alcoholism. After that I made myself stay away from the stuff."

To my surprise, the psychologist gave me an encouraging smile. "I congratulate you for that," he said, and I felt he meant it.

Nevertheless, I decided he had missed the point of my coming to see him. I was sure that I had wasted my time and money. However, I had failed to take into account the wheels that were turning behind the shrewd eyes.

"I will try to hypnotize you the next time you come," he said, much to my surprise. "But you should know that not everyone can be successfully hypnotized," he added. "It is important that you understand that, by itself, hypnosis has only a temporary effect. You need a broader therapy to solve your problems."

His shrewd eyes locked into mine. "I will try to hypnotize you because you might never seek professional help again if I don't. You may or may not be a good subject for hypnosis, but I think you might be willing to accept the behavioral therapy I recommend if you can get hypnosis off your mind."

That was smart of him, I thought, to know that I'd never come back if he refused to give hypnosis a try.

"There's something I want to check out before I let you go. Sit back and try to relax," he commanded. I leaned back into the chair without relaxing.

"Okay, now take a deep breath and let it out slowly. Good!"

He lowered his voice and spaced his words evenly. "Now close your eyes. Imagine that your eyelids are held together tightly by steel clamps. You can't open them now—no matter how hard you try. The clamps holding your eyelids together won't let you open them. Let yourself feel that." He paused.

I was surprised that I was actually visualizing my eyes held tightly shut by metal clamps.

"Now try to open them." The psychologist's voice sounded as if he were challenging me.

I tried to open my eyes. I couldn't. I twisted my face, trying to pull my forehead up. There was no way that I could open them. It was frightening!

"When I say 'now,' the clamps will drop off and you will be able to open your eyes easily." His voice commanded, "Now!"

My eyes sprang open as if helped by springs. The psychologist seemed to be surprised. Apparently he hadn't expected me to react to his suggestions as well as I did.

"Okay, it appears that you can be hypnotized," he said as the session ended.

I'm not easily fooled. As I made my next appointment, it occurred to me that he hadn't told me why he had agreed to hypnotize me. But it was clear to me that he'd decided to do it only because he was afraid I might become an alcoholic like my dad if he didn't.

At the shop the next day, I bragged to the guys that I was going to be hypnotized by a psychologist. I didn't expect Joe to laugh at the idea.

"That's too bad, Bill," he said, looking at me with pity. "Hypnosis is a fake. A couple of weeks ago I read in the newspaper that a college professor found that there was no scientific evidence that hypnosis works any better than a sugar pill against which he tested it. I'd stay away from it if I were you," he cautioned.

"My wife would never let me be brainwashed by a hypnotist!" Doug, who had been listening, added, "I advise you not to let some dumb shrink mess with your mind." He shuddered. "Besides," he whispered, moving closer to me, "my wife says hypnosis is a tool of the devil. You can be sure that no one in our church would fool with it."

I went home and looked up "hypnosis" in the dictionary. I read: "A trancelike condition, usually induced by another person, in which the subject is in a state of altered consciousness and responds, with certain limitations, to the suggestions of the hypnotist.''

I shut the dictionary, wondering how to cancel my appointment for next week. I decided to wait until the day before my hypnosis session was scheduled, then call the clinic and tell them I had changed my mind, or I was sick, or I would be out of town. But, in spite of my misgivings, I didn't cancel.

On the day of my appointment I just couldn't get myself into the mood to go. I was almost a half hour late. When I finally got to the psychologist's office, I hoped that there wouldn't be enough time left for me to have a session with him. But the receptionist smiled encouragingly when she saw me come in.

''You're lucky,'' she said. ''The doctor is running late and the next patient has canceled. He'll see you in a few minutes.'' I cursed under my breath.

Soon I found myself sitting in the recliner chair in the psychologist's office. Like the last time, I occupied only the first few inches of the seat.

The doctor was cheerful. ''Good to see you!'' he said smiling. He hadn't smiled when he saw me last week. Why was he smiling now?

"You shall have your wish to be hypnotized." He clasped and unclasped his hands—or was he rubbing them gleefully? I thought of the devil. "I know how much you want to be hypnotized," he muttered, consulting his notes. "However, don't try too hard to do it. Let nature take its course."

Let nature take its course? It sounded ominous.

"We shall first go through a brief relaxation exercise." I saw his eyes straying, for just a moment, to the wall clock on my right.

I was now leaning back in the recliner chair with my legs stretched out on the chair's extension. I did the breathing exercises as he instructed, but instead of feeling relaxed the way I was supposed to, I felt myself becoming more tense. Vaguely, I wondered if I could escape by getting up and running out of the office.

"There are various ways to induce the hypnotic trance," the psychologist began. "Each therapist uses the one that works best for him. I think you will like the method I use. I shall slowly count to ten." His voice was low, soothing. "As I count, you will very much want to close your eyes. You will find that you are becoming drowsy—more and more drowsy as you hear each number."

There seemed to be no doubt in his mind

that I would follow his directions. "With each number your eyes will get heavier and heavier and you will feel more and more comfortable. You will want very much to close your eyes and be even more comfortable. . . ."

I won't close them, I thought to myself, fighting his words.

"Of course, it all depends on you," his voice continued calmly. "If you wish, you can resist getting help." I pictured two shrewd eyes reading my thoughts.

"I've hypnotized hundreds of people safely," the voice went on. "None ever had an ill effect. But they cooperated fully. I've had a few clients who don't have the ability to relax. With them, I just had to end the session and send them home. Of course, we have to bill them just the same as we bill those who were successfully hypnotized. Let's begin. Take another deep breath and let it out slowly. Good. One, two, three, four, five, six. . . ."

I'll go along with it just to see what happens, I decided. Soon I began to feel my eyes getting heavy.

"You are now in a deep state of relaxation. You feel very, very comfortable." The psychologist's voice seemed to penetrate me.

I felt a pleasant darkness beginning to envelop me. It didn't seem to matter that a telephone was ringing somewhere. The traffic noise in the street below faded into a meaningless stream of distant sound.

"You are standing on six steps," his voice told me. "As you walk down each step you will go into a deeper and deeper state of relaxation."

His voice next told me that I was changing myself into a cloud floating in the sky. "You are not a happy cloud," he said. "You wish to rid yourself of the heavy burden of angry rain that you are holding within yourself. It's the anger within you that makes you feel depressed. But now you have the chance to rid yourself of it." He suggested gently, "Let go of it right now. . . ."

Something inside of me seemed to give way. I felt a torrent of angry red water rushing through me, then out of me, dropping down to earth.

The psychologist continued, "When you go home tonight you will be very loving to your wife. You will act toward her the way you did when you were first married. In return, she may make you very happy." His voice sounded almost seductive. Then it became louder, more insistent, "The posthypnotic suggestion I am about to give you will show that your hypnosis was successful."

"When you wake up you will want to raise your left arm to shoulder height," his voice told

me. "You will not be able to resist doing it!"
He added. "You will not be able to resist raising
your left arm to shoulder height as soon as you
wake up!" I heard the voice count, "One, two,
three, four, five. Wake up!"

My eyes opened slowly. I looked around. For
a moment I felt as if I were still floating. I
became aware of how pleasantly relaxed I felt.
My eyes focused on the psychologist across
from me. He was watching me intently—as if
waiting for something.

"Is there anything that you want to do now?"
he asked me after a few moments.

I shook my head, feeling very comfortable
and relaxed.

"There *is* something that you want to do right
now!" the psychologist insisted.

I was leaning back in the chair and wasn't in
the mood to play games of trivia with him.

"Don't you want to raise your left arm?" he
asked, frowning. I smiled and shook my head.

"Don't you want to do this?" he asked, raising his left arm shoulder high.

"No," I said, thinking it over carefully, "but
I'll do it if you want me to."

"Never mind," he replied, glancing at the
door as if to indicate that the session was over.

When I got home, I noticed that my wife

looked somehow different—more attractive than when I had said goodbye to her in the morning.

It had been a long time since we hit it off as well as we did that evening. As we undressed to go to bed, I was delighted to see a rare, tender look on my wife's face, and recognized its meaning. I felt myself responding with an excitement heightened by long deprivation. I paused for just a moment to give silent thanks to the psychologist who had hypnotized me.

My wife was already in bed, looking at me and smiling; I stood by my side of the bed in my pajamas with my left arm held up rigidly at shoulder height.

My wife stared at me in disbelief. ''You look ridiculous standing there like that!'' she said, turning away and pulling the covers over herself.

The tension in my arm slowly ebbed. A few minutes passed and my arm descended and again felt normal. With a surge of anger I listened to the soft, rhythmic sound of my wife's snoring.

## COMMENT:

*Bill's difficulty in social and occupational performance is typical of a Passive Aggressive Personality*

*Disorder. This disorder is widely distributed in the general population, but is somewhat more common among men than women. Persons having this disorder feel hostility directly but express it indirectly. Resistance to authority, distaste for sustained work, failure to cooperate, and the habit of deliberately arriving late for appointments are passive ways used to express anger.*

*Bill expected hypnosis to be an easy way to rid himself of his problems. The psychologist knew that people with personality disorders are frequently unable to accept the suggestions necessary to achieve a trancelike state. To the psychologist's surprise, when tested at the first session, Bill demonstrated that he was capable of following the suggestions. The psychologist expected Bill's hostility to interfere with the hypnosis induction process. It is not always easy to determine, without testing, who is and who is not susceptible to hypnosis.*

*Bill's underlying resistance, held in check during trance state, surfaced when the psychologist gave him a posthypnotic suggestion. The unconscious mind monitors hypnotic activity. When alerted, it enables the hypnotized subject to reject or delay the implementation of specific suggestions. When that occurs, it naturally disappoints the hypnotist, since he is unable to confirm that genuine hypnosis occurred. Frustrating a person in authority is grist for the passive aggressive's mill. By delaying the posthypnotic suggestion given him by the psychologist, Bill was able to defy him and have the last laugh—almost!*

*Eric found a purpose in life by joining the Avengers. He was intelligent and enthusiastic, and it wasn't surprising that he became a leader in the group. When he was chosen to officiate at the meeting that inaugurated PHASE TWO of the Avengers' program, Eric wanted to wear his grandfather's military sword. Family tradition was important to Eric, but more important was the enduring love he maintained for his mother, who had died in childbirth. As we all know, the power of love can lead to unexpected behavior.*

*Eric's story is not an account of events that actually occurred, but a psychological reconstruction of circumstances that could lead to the scenario described.*

# ERIC:
# The Avenger

The dozen or so Avengers Bill had recruited at our high school had come to our meeting. We played volley ball on the courts behind Bill's house and then gathered on the patio for Cokes and sandwiches. The patio was large enough to seat our group comfortably. It was lined by a row of trees that provided shade and privacy. The boundaries of Bill's ranch extended beyond the trees to include a stretch of hilly terrain that was well suited for practicing our drills and war games. When it was covered by deep snow in the winter, it was perfect for testing our ability to cope with the weather and survive.

I thought how different we were from guys who had no goals in life. In my gut I felt the approval we had for each other. It was something I had always longed for—approval from others my own age. Our feelings for each other came from our willingness to take risks to achieve our common goal.

I remember the day I first met Bill. He was waiting in the high school parking lot after school let out. I was with two guys from my class. He came up to us and started talking about the danger that he saw ahead for the white race. He told us that environmentalists were protecting eagles and whales. It was wrong, he said, that no one was protecting the white race that was endangered by outsiders like Asians, blacks, and Jews. Then he explained that he had come to the high school to look for some guys with guts who would be willing to help him save the white race from becoming extinct. He said, "You're the kind of men I have been looking for." Then he invited us to visit his ranch which was a few miles out of town. He promised to help us gain the skills we would need to save the white race from destruction by outsiders.

That was a year and a half ago. Before then, I had been drifting around and never thought about the white race. I had often been lonely, but when I tried to make friends with other guys, I didn't connect. Sports didn't interest me, I wasn't into experimenting with drugs, and the clubs at school were boring. That made me an outsider. Bill's invitation to join the Avengers came at a time when I wanted to get involved in something that would give my life some kind of direction. The others who accepted Bill's invitation may have felt as I did, but after a while, many of them stopped coming to the ranch. Only about a quarter of the guys he had recruited, including me, remained to attend the meetings. We successfully survived the probation period and took an oath of loyalty to the white race and the organization. We then became fully accepted Avengers.

I recall that on my first visit to the ranch, I realized that Bill wasn't poor—far from it! He owned a large house and some smaller buildings on several acres of land. He told us that he made his living as a construction electrician. He must have worked on a lot of big projects to afford the house, buy gear for our war games, and pay for the audio-visual equipment we used in what he called the "war room." It was the largest room in Bill's house and had probably been made by knocking out a wall between two smaller rooms. It was big enough for the talks and instructions that didn't require field exercises or target practice.

In the war room there were shelves filled with books on the white race, including some on Hitler and the Nazis. A few of these were even in their original German editions. A collection of sabers hung on another wall, some with swastikas on their hilts. There were also a couple of American sabers that dated back to the Civil war. World War II guns used by the Germans and Italians were displayed in a cabinet behind sliding glass doors. The chairs in the war room were arranged facing a blackboard and the large screen which was used for projecting slides Bill used to illustrate his talks. We moved the chairs out of the way when our program called for karate practice.

Bill kept warning us that unless we took action soon, nonwhites would overrun the United States and make white people second-class citizens. He repeated this so often that our concern for the white race became a living part of us. He outlined our mission as threefold: rid our country of Jewish influence, prevent blacks from infiltrating our government, and stop the immigration of Asians into the United States.

Using slides, newspaper reports, and his personal research, he showed us how the Jews were manipulating our government and our financial institutions for their own advantage. He said that the Aryan race had been stupid in opposing Hitler's solution to the ''Jewish problem.''

Bill and his son, Dave, provided all of our training. Bill is a strong man with broad shoulders. Dave seemed slight by comparison. But Dave is no weakling when it comes to teaching us how to unite and fight to save the white race. Older than most of us, Dave also does the paperwork that keeps us in contact with other groups in the United States that have concerns and goals similar to ours.

A couple of weeks ago Bill called a special meeting. When we were all together in the war room he announced that at our next regular meeting he would mark the start of Phase Two of our mission. Phase One had consisted of letting the Jews know that the Avengers had them in their sights. We did this by spraying swastikas and anti-Jewish slogan on walls of their synagogues, schools, and shops. In Phase Two we would begin the real attack.

Only Bill, Dave, an Avenger named Paul, and I knew that we were making a bomb. We spent many hours in Bill's workshop studying how to do it. We figured it out by following the instructions in one of Bill's books. The book listed all of the materials needed, and illustrated step by step how to make different kinds of bombs. Paul had been selected because he could repair anything that was ever broken. He was always tinkering with something mechanical. After we learned that Paul had his own chemistry lab in the basement of his home, we called him our "genius." We felt we could rely on Paul's know-how to put the bomb together right. He cleverly redesigned the bomb's detonating mechanism to give us the options any situation might demand. These options ranged from detonating it immediately to delaying detonation for up to twelve hours. The four of us swore to maintain secrecy, and even among ourselves, would refer to the bomb only as the "Holy Grail."

All the Avengers took turns conducting the ceremony with which we began our regular meetings. We started with "God Bless America" and followed with a pledge never to reveal our activities to anyone. Next week it was my turn to conduct the ceremony. I was proud when Bill told me that he had chosen our next meeting's opening ceremony as the time to share our secret with the other Avengers. Bill wanted all of the Avengers to know that the bomb was ready so that all of us could claim equal responsibility and credit for the results of its explosion. Bill planned that I would carry in the bomb and hold it high for all to see during the ceremony. He would then reveal his plans for setting it off in the largest synagogue in town at the upcoming Jewish holiday.

I was grateful that Bill had selected me to introduce the "Holy Grail" to the others. I often wished that I had a father like Bill instead of the drunk that I call, "Dad." The only good thing that you can say about my father is that he is a pure Aryan. It was bad luck for me when he married Sophia after my mother died. Her family comes from somewhere in southern Europe. I'm glad that she isn't my real mother. Some people think I look like Sophia because my hair is dark like hers. Dad told me that my real mother, Martha, died when I was born. Dad must have hated her because he never mentions her. Once I asked him to show me some pictures of my mother, and he told me that he didn't have any. When I think of my mother I always feel sad and guilty that she died while giving me life. Sometimes I try to imagine her as still alive, loving me and proud of me.

It didn't seem very long before the day came around that I was to conduct the opening ceremony at our meeting. With a jolt I remembered that it would mark the beginning of Phase Two. I had been given the role of revealing the "Holy Grail" to the others at the start of the ceremony. Bill suggested that I should create an impression in presenting the bomb that, as he put it, "the Avengers would never forget!" I recalled that when I was a small boy, Dad had shown me a saber that had belonged to my grandfather. I knew Dad kept it in the attic. I pictured myself proudly wearing it at the ceremony. I decided that after revealing the "Holy Grail" I would flourish the saber and shout "Death to the Jews!"

I took my flashlight and crept upstairs to the attic to look for the saber. It was summer, and I was sweating. I searched all over for the saber, but found only half empty boxes of old clothing, electric wires, and plumbing parts. Angrily, I thought that Dad probably had sold it to get money for whiskey. As I started to crawl back toward the trap door I saw a cardboard box I hadn't noticed before. It didn't seem as dusty as the others. A cracked three-legged stool stood next to it. A few discarded flashlight batteries lay nearby, leading me to think that whoever came up here spent a good amount of time sitting on the stool with a flashlight looking at what was in the box. I opened the box hoping I might find an old gun that Grandpa may have worn in the war, or at least some of his war medals. I could pin them on my shirt to help make the ceremony dramatic. When I opened it I found only a collection of old letters and photographs. Disappointed, I untied the string that held them together and looked at the photograph that was on top. My eyes were drawn to the words written at the bottom of the picture—"To my darling, from Martha."

I stopped breathing as I looked at the beautiful face of my mother! With trembling hands, I turned the picture over. On the back of the photograph I recognized my father's handwriting, "Martha, sweetheart! I will never forget you, not in life nor in death." It seemed to me that he must have written this after my mother died. I stared at my mother's grey eyes and brown hair almost feeling that she was still alive. My finger lovingly traced the lines of her delicate chin. Then, not knowing what I was doing, I kissed the face of my mother again and again, saying, "Mother, Mother, Mother." I don't know how long I sat there.

I read a few of the love letters my dad and mom had written to each other. For the first time in my life I felt some sympathy for my father. I realized then that the loss of his beautiful wife may well have contributed to his becoming an alcoholic. One of the letters I read mentioned some family problem caused by my parents planning to get married. The next letter explained it. In my father's handwriting I read, "Martha darling, it doesn't matter to me that you are Jewish. The only thing that counts is that you are the sweetest, loveliest, and most wonderful girl in all the world." I put the letter down. Something in me froze. I was half Jewish!

Moving like I was in a dream, I climbed out

of the attic and quickly shut the trapdoor behind me. I rushed to the bathroom to look at myself in the mirror. As I stared at the reflection of my face, the thought rushed through my head, "You're looking at a *Jew*!"

I examined my nose carefully for the signs Bill had told us were typical of Jews. I sighed with relief. "They'll never find out!" I told myself. Nothing on my face looked Jewish to me. But the longer I stared at my reflection in the mirror, the more I imagined a hint of what I had been taught was the typical Jewish look. I turned my head away from the mirror, closed my eyes tightly, and took a deep breath. When I looked into the mirror again, I saw only the regular features of an Aryan. The picture of my mother did not look like Bill had described Jews. The more I thought about it, the more certain I became that my mother must have been mistaken in thinking she was Jewish.

That night I tried to keep my mind on tomorrow's ceremony. This kept me turning and tossing long after I went to bed. At last I must have fallen asleep because I dreamed I saw my mother worshiping in the synagogue that the Avengers planned to bomb. I heard the bomb explode. I saw my mother crushed as parts of the ceiling fell on her. Her scream was like a knife blade ripping through my chest. I awoke shouting, "Mother! Mother!" I was dripping with sweat. In the darkness, no one could see my tears.

I was unable to go back to sleep. Some unwanted questions began to creep into my mind. Didn't all of us humans originate in Africa, as scientists claim? Weren't there African-Americans, who the Avengers called "inferior," who had demonstrated outstanding abilities and who held jobs of national importance? Didn't I read somewhere that some of the earliest civilizations began in Asia, and wasn't there a TV special that claimed that Asians were among the smartest and hardest-working people in our country? Why did Bill associate Jews only with making money when they are also well-known scientists, doctors, and musicians? When the Avengers sang "God Bless America," didn't they know that a Jew had written the music and the words? Then the question I had pushed out of my mind since I had joined the Avengers returned with full force—"Do we Avengers need to hate non-whites and Jews? Or do we simply need to *hate*?"

AT THE MEETING:

The meeting of the Avengers was called to order. Attendance was taken and Bill announced that everyone was present. He stepped aside so that Eric could take over. Eric rose and stood erect before the upturned faces. The muscles of his face were tight. His mouth was a thin line. He looked appropriately grim for the initiation of Phase Two. Accompanied by cheers, Eric carefully removed the bomb from its wooden box and raised it high for all to see. Ignoring Bill's look of alarm, Eric reached for the detonator.

"This is the "Holy Grail," Eric shouted. "Take it as a salute to you from an avenger!" The cheering was drowned out by the deafening sound of the explosion.

NEWSPAPER ARTICLE:

The newspapers's lead article read: "A group of young white racists and their leader were killed when a homemade bomb presented at their meeting accidentally detonated. The explosion was devastating. There were no survivors. The FBI is investigating further.

## COMMENT:

*Racism is a current psychosocial problem that statistics show is growing worldwide. Racists interpret the actions of specific groups of people as dangerous and deliberately aimed at themselves or at those with whom they identify. The current Diagnostic Manual of the American Psychiatric Association states that people with this disorder "intensely and narrowly search for confirmation of their expectations. There is no appreciation of the total context.*

Their final conclusion is usually precisely what they expected in the first place.''

Racists may be personable, present themselves well, and be warm and friendly toward people not in the specific categories they identify with threat or danger. There are several secondary gains to be found in racism. It leads to a bonding that creates feeling of intense togetherness with like-minded people. These persons enhance their self-images by viewing themselves as dedicated to a worthy cause in which they fervently believe and for which they are willing to make unusual sacrifices.

This attitude helps them gain additional adherents who may have any of a number of dissatisfactions with their lives. They may lack companionship and seek ''a purpose for living,'' as Eric did. Participation in hate-group activism offers those engaged in it a self-enhancing comradeship. Its militancy lends racial hate an aura of manliness and strength. That is why those who engage in racially motivated sabotage are almost invariably unrelenting.

Nevertheless, sometimes among such groups there is a person like Eric who has a lingering doubt about the justification of the stand taken by the hate group to which he/she belongs. This doubt is repressed as long as he is affiliated with such a group, but it may be propelled to the surface under unusual circumstances. The discovery that his mother was Jewish gave Eric only two choices—denial or explosive action.

*She came to the counselor for one reason only—to avoid losing her job. She didn't like him at first. The chemistry between them was wrong, and rapport seemed out of reach. Had she made a mistake in coming to him? She was almost sure she had until he discovered—one might say—the roots of her problem. After that she got much more than the advice for which she had come. Far too much more!*

# SHARON:
# My Father's Mask

Session 1, June 1: I felt uneasy as the counselor's gray eyes, enlarged by thick bifocals, scrutinized me. It was my first visit. I had come to see him because I was having serious problems at my job. I sat stiffly at the edge of the recliner chair in his office.

"And how long were you an airline hostess, Sharon?" he asked me.

"You mean flight attendant. That's a common error. Fourteen years," I replied. My mind flashed back to those almost forgotten days. How exciting they were at first! They became less so as time went by.

"Now you have a problem getting along with

your boss?'' The thick lenses were aimed at the form I had filled out in the waiting room.

''But you must have been well liked earlier to have gotten promoted to your present position,'' he added, reading further.

I decided that if the round-faced man with the grey-flecked hair sitting across from me was attempting to win me over with logic, he was failing. I had come to consult him reluctantly. I needed advice because my job was on the line and I couldn't afford to lose it. I found his name in the yellow pages of the phone book under ''Counselors.'' He listed his specialty as helping people with ''vocational and marital adjustment problems.'' I had expected to see someone suave and masterful. He did not fit my expectations. He was rotund and past middle age. His voice was pitched a trifle higher than I found comfortable.

''I was promoted ahead of the others because I worked harder than they did,'' I said with a shrug, trying to imply that I considered it irrelevant.

''And you were better looking?''

I was taken aback. ''No, I just worked harder, was always on time, put up with more crap and all that.''

''And, at that time, you got along well with your supervisors?''

I nodded. "I didn't complain, kept my mouth shut, and did as I was told."

"Did as you were told?" he repeated.

Was there a touch of sarcasm in his voice? I couldn't be sure. I decided it was my insecurity that made me think so.

"When you say that you did what you were told to do, are you referring to your duties on the job or to more than that?"

I shot a quick glance at him. The counselor's voice had been casual, not probing. "My duties were varied," I said, feeling myself becoming defensive.

"Sex?" he asked in an offhand manner.

I didn't like the direction the interview was taking. Nevertheless, I answered his questions so that I could get the advice I needed.

"When I first started working for the airline, there were some flight attendants who acted as if sex was expected of them," I explained. "They were wrong of course."

"After I left home I began to experiment with having sex," I admitted, thinking that this was what he wanted to know.

"But you didn't have to be involved in sex to keep your job." It was not a question.

"Technically, no." The thought that I never had to come back to see the counselor again crossed my mind and made me feel more re-laxed.

He seemed to ignore the obvious lack of rap-port between us. ''Did you think you needed to have affairs to be happy?'' he continued.

''It was happiness, not sex that I was after,'' I told him. I hoped that he would be aware of the annoyance in my voice. ''At that time all I wanted to do was to get away from home,'' I said, recalling how miserable home had been. ''After I beat the competition and was accepted for flight attendant training, I thought I had found happiness. It wasn't very long before I realized that I was unlikely to find it on my job. At first, I could not accept that. I worked hard to deceive myself into thinking that I was happy. When I could no longer pretend and finally ad-mitted that I was unhappy, I kept it to myself. No one would have guessed how miserable I was by what I said or did. I put on a show, laughed a lot. Everyone thought I was having a ball.'' My eyes strayed from the counselor's face to the abstract paintings hanging on the wall behind him. I hoped that he was not going to pursue this subject further.

Again he consulted the form which I had filled out in his waiting room prior to seeing him. ''And then the airline promoted you and gave you much more responsibility. And after

that you found that you were even more unhappy than before?''

I nodded.

''Have you ever thought about why that
might be?''

''I don't know,'' I replied, feeling no emo-
tion. I didn't tell him that I didn't really care.

''I didn't like continuing to pretend,'' I told
him after a few moments of thought. ''I may be
more openly depressed now, but at least I'm not
lying to myself anymore. I can tolerate this
since most of the time I'm not really deeply
depressed, and some days are better than others.'' Again I wished that the counselor would
get off the track he had taken. I hadn't come to
see him to discuss my depression. I'd come to
him for practical advice on how to save my job
at the airline. Then it occurred to me that he
might need more background information in order to assess the difficulty I was having on my
job. I decided to become more cooperative.

''Did anything significant happen in your life
while you were a flight attendant?''

''I got married. It didn't last.''

''It didn't last?''

''Three years was enough for me.''

''Three years was enough for you?'' he
echoed.

''My ex-husband was a baby. I had enough

passengers who were babies. I didn't need another one at home.'' I felt a shudder as I recalled my former husband's face. Once I had thought it handsome and boyish. In retrospect I recalled it as coarse and repulsive.

''Were there children in your marriage?''

''No. I didn't want children. Perhaps if my own childhood had been happier, things would have been different. Anyway I didn't want children with Frank.''

''You mentioned your childhood. Do you wish to talk about it.''

I started to say ''no,'' but something made me blurt out, ''I was very unhappy! Dad was the boss in our home. From the day I was four he called me his 'only sweetheart.' My mother was a nonentity. She was just there, never counting, never making decisions. I had two brothers who were sport fans from the day they were born. Their minds were outside of our home and so were their lives. I got along with them okay. They treated me special because I was a girl and because Dad wouldn't let anyone mess with me. Dad spoiled me rotten. There wasn't a thing I wanted that he didn't try to get me. In contrast, poor Mom got nothing—not even thanks for cooking, doing the housekeeping, and also working part-time. On the other hand, Dad always did whatever he wanted to do. He seemed to care only about himself.''

"How would you describe your father?"

"Crude, a bore, selfish, perverted." There was the familiar shudder. I looked at the counselor defiantly, expecting disapproval.

He sat with his hands folded; an inscrutable expression was on his face and his thoughts seemed turned inward. He reminded me now of a displaced Buddha.

Speaking slowly, in a lowered voice, he asked, "Did your mother know what was going on between you and your father?"

I felt the color rising to my cheeks. He knows, *he knows!* For a moment I wondered how the bastard had learned that my father had forced me to have sex with him all the years I was growing up. Then I realized that he'd read the truth between the lines of what I had said. The last thing I wanted was for him to dig up what I had so firmly kept out of my mind. Damn him! I only wanted him to suggest strategies to save my job! Again, I regretted having come to see him.

"We needn't talk about it now," the counselor said, seeming to read my thoughts. "You don't ever have to talk about it if you don't want to," he added, nodding reassuringly.

Session 2, June 8th: "What do you want to talk about today?" the counselor asked. Didn't he know that I wanted him to tell me how I could keep from getting into more trouble on my job?

"I want to talk about a demotion I've been threatened with at work," I said, determined to stick to the subject. "I refuse to accept it because it isn't fair. I do my job as it should be done, and Stanley, my boss, can't deny it. He claims that I can't get along with people." I felt anger flaring up.

"As a stewardess, how did you get along with the passengers?"

Was he avoiding my job problems again? "As a flight attendant" I said,—why couldn't he call me that?—"I got along better than most of the others." It was true.

"And with your supervisors?"

"I had no problems with them, then."

"And now, in your present job as a loading supervisor, your boss is upset because you object to the changes in the loading procedure which he suggested?"

"Yes. The loading procedures are my personal responsibility. They must conform to government regulations, and I'm held accountable by the FAA. But it isn't that alone. I've given in to others too often in my life!" I felt tension building up in me as I was talking. "I decided to oppose Stanley's interference," I said, feeling self-righteous. I didn't tell the counselor that I wouldn't really have been breaking any rules if I had consented to doing things the way Stanley had suggested. Stanley and I had been quibbling over basically minor changes.

"For once I had made up my mind to stick to my guns and not give in to others," I said defiantly.

I was surprised to find myself wanting the counselor to support my view. "What I really resented," I continued, "was Stanley's intrusion into my bailiwick! He is my boss only in the limited way that pertains to certain specific duties, not to all of them." The intensity of my resentment was rising. I took a breath and sank deeper into the roomy client chair.

He did not reply immediately. I relaxed in the silence that followed. After several minutes the counselor asked, "Do you think that Stanley is hostile to you because you are a woman in what he may regard as a man's job?"

"You may well be right," I said, wondering why that had not previously occurred to me. However, I felt that there must be more to it than that.

He looked straight at me. "Could it be that not having sex with him might be a reason he's down on you?"

I was startled. "He doesn't need me for that!" I replied quickly.

"But you're good-looking," the counselor continued. I hated him for saying that.

"There are enough good-looking women around where I work who are more than willing to have sex with him." My annoyance toward the counselor was mounting. However, I went on, "I am responsible for keeping the records the government wants maintained on the loading procedures. I'd be the first one blamed if Stanley's suggestions for changing them didn't work out." I knew I was exaggerating. There would be no real basis for blaming me. Talking about my job difficulties had become tiresome and confusing. I sighed.

The counselor seemed to ignore my distaste for further discussion of the matter. "Can you tell me what your boss could do to make you like working with him more?" he asked.

"I want him to keep his nose out of my business!" I flared. "Stanley's position does not give him the right to interfere with how I do things as long as the company approves! The thought of his trying to dominate me makes me furious!" I found myself shouting and breathing hard.

"I don't blame you for being upset about it," the counselor said soothingly. At last! I thought. I had been waiting for reassurance from him from the first day I came to see him.

Abruptly he changed the subject. "Your marriage lasted three years?"

"That is all I could take," I told him. "My husband couldn't hold a job. He was good-looking, tall, and all that. That's what attracted me to him at first." I paused. "No, it was more than that," I recalled. "It was that he needed my help in order to be able to function. Helpless men have always appealed to me," I said, frowning when I realized how ridiculous that sounded.

"So after you were married you changed your mind about wanting a helpless husband?" The question made me realize that it was more than Frank's dependence on me that had made my marriage impossible.

"Well, it was also because he was crude, a bore, and selfish." The words slipped out automatically as if I had practiced saying them.

"In regard to sex?" the counselor asked. He sighed wearily. I got the impression that he had become as tired of discussing the subject as I had.

I nodded.

It seemed to me now that talking about sex made him feel uncomfortable. I realized that he was questioning me about it only because he had to in order to get to the root of my problem. For a fleeting moment I wondered if the man facing me suffered from sexual problems of his own. If this were true, he and I would have something in common. The idea made me feel warmer toward him.

The counselor's voice brought me back to my own problems. "You described your husband as 'crude, a bore, and selfish,' " he reminded me. "Are you aware that earlier you used the identical words to describe your father?"

I had never seen the connection before! For a moment I felt disbelief. Could it be that sex with Frank had revolted me because it reminded me of what my father had done to me when I was a child? Somehow it seemed to fit. I could see it now. A rush of pain swept over me. I found myself crying, and the tears seemed to bring indescribable relief.

I looked at the counselor through my tears, realizing then that I had misjudged him. He was much smarter than I had given him credit for. And kinder too, I thought, when he placed a comforting hand on my shoulder.

Gradually, I found myself no longer resenting the counseling sessions. I began to look forward to them. I was grateful that I had found someone with whom I could be open about myself. I felt comforted and protected in his presence.

I was now beginning to gain insights into myself that never would have been possible before counseling. During subsequent sessions I began to understand that my resentment toward Stanley harked back to my memories of my father's sexual advances when I was a child. In time I realized how much my father's sexual abuse had warped my life. I could see now that, symbolically, I was trying to avenge myself for what my father had done to me. It seems that I felt compelled to punish the father-images in my life—my former husband, and now Stanley. It all became crystal clear. But best of all was the confidence I had gained that now no one could ever take advantage of me again.

"Your problem, Sharon, is," the counselor said, looking directly at me and speaking meaningfully, "that you never had sex with love."

There it was! I have never had sex with love! I repeated that amazing statement to myself. Could this be the key to the door of my happiness that had for so long been locked? It occurred to me that as a flight attendant I had still been working out another need—to be accepted. My father had taught me that I had to earn his acceptance by giving in to his sexual demands. The angry and rejecting part of me dared not emerge until I had gained stature and self-esteem. As an adult holding a managerial position, I thought I had at last found the courage to assert myself. But without the necessary insights, I had been driven to assert myself inappropriately. Now I could admit to others that I would not have broken any regulations if I had followed Stanley's suggestions. Instead, the shortcuts he recommended would have made life a little easier for everyone.

Now, when something makes me angry I can ask myself, "Am I unconsciously responding to what my father did to me? When I realize that this is unreasonable, my emotions, quickly become more appropriate. The counselor had cautioned me that my emotional scars would never fully heal. But now they no longer need to interfere with my life.

I asked myself, "Is happiness at last within my grasp?" Silently came the answer. "Yes." And with this answer my heart turned toward my counselor in gratitude. He gave me liberation from the confused emotions which remained after my father had betrayed my trust by violating my body. My eyes found those of the counselor's. For the first time I realized that he looked years younger than his actual age. His face sensitively reflected his concern for me.

"Sex without love has done this to you," he told me in a voice that gave those words a deep meaning, "and that is why sex with love will provide you with what you have been looking for." He walked over to where I sat and gently put his arms around me.

September 3rd: Those weeks were heavenly

hell. And now that it is over, the heaven has slid out of those weeks leaving only the hell behind. In my tortured dreams I see my counselor again. He appears in them as a monster wearing a mask of my father's face.

December 1st: (Related by Sharon's former counselor)

I felt uneasy as the psychologist's blue eyes scrutinized me. He knew why I had lost my license to practice. I sat stiffly at the edge of the patients' recliner chair. It seemed to me that I could feel his disapproval. I took a breath and began to relax as I decided to trust his professional objectivity.

## COMMENT:

*Professionals in the mental health field are aware that many of their clients are needy and this tends to make them vulnerable to suggestions. Properly trained therapists know that some members of the opposite sex may go through a stage of becoming infatuated with them in the course of their therapy. It is not unusual for a lonely client, having difficulty coping, to feel that their therapist is the only person who is concerned about them. At that point in the therapy a client may even fall in love with his/her therapist.*

*Usually it isn't difficult for a mental health specialist to remain uninvolved romantically when this*

happens. Over time, clients are inclined to appreciate their therapist's lack of reciprocity to their romantic overtures. When infatuation has occurred,
success in therapy requires the client to "fall out of
love," and in so doing, gain independence from
the therapist. Continuing emotional dependence is a
mark of failure for all involved.

Often, in the popular psychological literature,
"gaining insight" is equated with getting cured.
However, "insights" can lead to misconceptions
even if they are quite genuine. Thinking that she
had gained insight gave Sharon a false sense of
security. It took more than knowing that her relationships with some men "symbolized her exploitation by her father." That knowledge failed to save
her from further exploitation by the man "who wore
her father's mask."

*There are many shy people in the world. There are also many who are confused about their feelings toward members of the opposite sex. However, there may be much more than meets the eye to both confusion and shyness. Sometimes, they have tangled roots, and confusion may deepen when these roots are unearthed. Carol found that out after much trial and error—mostly error.*

# CAROL:
# "Insight" Wasn't Enough

"For me, legs are just legs," I said, facing the woman therapist I had come to consult.

"But, of course, for men they are more than that," I told her, "because when I wear short skirts men look at my legs. After I have walked by they turn around and keep looking."

The therapist glanced at my legs. I had them crossed.

"You have shapely legs," she said casually.

"My problem is," I continued, "when men look at me it makes me feel uncomfortable. But when they pass by and don't seem to notice me, I resent it."

My eyes swept over the therapist's short hair,

her conservative dress, and the sensible walking shoes she was wearing.

"I've tried not using makeup and wearing clothes that are not revealing," I said. "I found that it doesn't make me feel any better."

"You don't want men to notice you and yet you are annoyed when they don't. That's why you came to see me?"

"Yes," I admitted, beginning to feel foolish.

The therapist seemed to be thinking this over. "In other ways how do you feel about having contact with men?"

"Maybe there is something wrong with me. I'm afraid of men. I don't want any man to touch me. I don't think I could stand it. Yet—and this is what bothers me—I often daydream that men are holding me tight in their arms."

"What kinds of men are in your daydreams?"

"At different times there are different kinds of men. Sometimes they're dressed in business suits, and other times they wear worn work clothes."

I watched the therapist write something on her pad. I repressed an urge to ask her what she had written.

"I have always been shy in the presence of men," I continued. "Even when I was a small child I was afraid of them. I really had no reason to be," I said, feeling defensive.

The therapist's eyes again were on her pad. "Did you have friendships with boys when you were in high school?"

"I used to talk with some of the guys about teachers and school subjects. As soon as they became too friendly, I ignored them. They thought I was stuck up. That's why I wasn't popular with boys. The girls in high school were interested in dating and clothes. I had nothing in common with them."

"Was it sex that you were afraid of?" the therapist asked.

"It scares me to think about it." Now she knew why I had really come to see her.

"Yet you daydream that men are holding you in their arms?"

"I know that it doesn't make sense. I thought that maybe you could help me understand why I am this way."

The therapist shifted her chair a little closer to me.

"Did you ever have a frightening experience with a man?"

I shook my head.

"Were you sexually molested as a child?"

I had asked myself that question several

times. "As far as I can remember, nothing like that ever happened to me. Once I asked Mom if anyone had done anything that might have frightened me when I was a kid. She said that she didn't know of anything that would have made me afraid of anyone. My dad and my brother loved and respected me. They wouldn't think of hurting me. When I was a teenager, Mom worried that my shyness might mean that there was something wrong with me. She wanted me to go for counseling, but I refused. I didn't want to talk to anyone about it. Anyway, Mom thought I'd outgrow being shy."

"Do you have any relatives who are very shy?"

Why did the therapist ask that I wondered. Could I have inherited some kind of defect?

"Neither my brother nor my parents are shy. My two aunts are anything but afraid of people! They are life-of-the-party types. I have some relatives living along the coast, but we haven't been in touch. As far as I know, none of them are shy."

The therapist turned a page in a folder. "I'm looking at the results of your medical exam. According to your doctor, you are physically okay." She seemed to be thinking. The pen in her hand drummed on her desk.

"She's stumped!" I told myself. For some

odd reason, the thought made me feel good, and yet, frightened.

"Perhaps, I was born to be lesbian?" I asked her.

The therapist raised an eyebrow. "Your fantasy life doesn't fit that."

Silently I agreed. I have never been physically attracted to a woman. Years ago I thought I might try something like that just to see what would happen. But when I pictured myself in the arms of a woman, it seemed no more exciting than being draped in a blanket. On the other hand, imagining myself held tightly in the arms of a man excited, and at the same time, upset me. I was sure I would never let it happen. I wondered what the therapist was writing.

"There is probably something dormant in your mind that you are repressing," she said after a while. Psychoanalysis may help uncover it. But even short-term psychoanalysis takes time, perhaps six or more months of weekly visits. Would you be willing to commit yourself to that?"

Psychoanalysis? I hadn't counted on anything like that. My eyes strayed to the green couch along the office wall. In my mind I saw a woman reclining on it. There were tears in her eyes as she recalled a horrible experience in her childhood. Suddenly, the couch took the shape of an operating table. I saw myself stretched out on it—anesthetized. The therapist's gloved hands were probing for a malignant tumor deep within my brain. I seemed to be fighting for my breath when a locked door suddenly sprang open in my mind. Through the door I saw Grandpa bending over me in bed. He was saying, "Good night, dear—I'll kill you if you ever tell anyone what we did!"

"I don't want to be psychoanalyzed," I heard myself shouting. I was sure the therapist now thought I was insane.

A deep breath helped. "At present I have no need to be involved with men," I told her, wishing that the therapy session were over. "I have a bookkeeping job in a firm where people leave me alone as long as I do my work. I've thought of getting a cat or a dog for company, but I decided I don't need a pet. I don't need anyone! I'm okay."

"So why did you come to see me?"

"I want to know why I'm so mixed up."

"Getting to the root of that will take more time than you are willing to give."

I shrugged. I had wasted the lady's time in coming to see her, but I had gained a frightening insight. So that was it. Grandfather had molested me and threatened to kill me if I told on him. I had buried the memory of it so it wouldn't haunt me. The missing piece of my life's puzzle had fallen into my lap. At last I knew why I feared men. I now had gained the insight I needed to be able to help myself. I felt a surge of enthusiasm and hope. On the way out, I told the receptionist that I did not plan to have another session.

The following weeks I spent hours in the library and in bookstores reading psychology books. I enrolled in a course in personal adjustment at the community college.

I did my best to apply what I had learned from my reading and in my class. At first it was exciting. But after a few months, the excitement faded. As more time passed I had to admit that I felt more miserable than before. I found it difficult to concentrate and was increasingly anxious and irritable. It upset me that knowing what my problem was hadn't helped me cope with it. Wasn't insight the key to self-understanding? Maybe I needed another flashback to get more details. I turned my thoughts back to when I was a child and tried to remember all I could about my grandfather.

At first, my mind was blank. I couldn't even remember what my grandfather had looked like. As I let my mind drift, I pictured my grandfather tiptoeing into my bedroom. Strangely, in my memory, he looked young, then old, then young again as if he were several different persons. I shuddered as I thought that I felt one of his hands roughly holding me down while his other hand moved over my body again and again. I pictured him finally leaving and warning me that he would kill me if I ever told anyone what had happened. I could remember crying myself to sleep after he left. When I woke up my stomach muscles were tied into knots.

I wondered if I could now link my second flashback to the mixed-up feelings I had toward men. I hoped that by reliving, in a dream state, the frightening recollections of my grandfather molesting me I would be able to expel the pent-up resentment from my unconscious mind. My studies of psychology made me believe that this could happen. I thought that then, perhaps, I could really straighten myself out. My enthusiasm returned, but not for long. Instead of feeling better as I had expected, I found my anxiety and self-doubt increasing after I'd had the second flashback. I began to regret that I hadn't told the therapist about my flashback in her office. I had been foolish to think that I could cure myself by gaining insight into what had caused my problem.

Nevertheless, my effort may have accomplished something positive. I noticed that my feeling toward men had changed in some subtle, indescribable way. I no longer had fantasies of being held in a man's arms. Was this progress,

I wondered. I decided that it was enough to continue exploring my feelings further. For that, I needed a man. I needed to be held in his arms so that I could test myself. Some of my enthusiasm returned when I convinced myself that the time for giving up had not yet arrived.

At the office, my boss had recently moved me to a desk near a man named Jim, who was about my age. I was glad to learn that he was married, but I knew that this didn't stop many men from trying to date. I hoped that Jim wouldn't be one of those.

When I was at my new desk, I wasn't surprised to find Jim's eyes straying in my direction. I noticed that if I turned toward him, he would look away quickly. Once his wife visited him at the office. She brought along their two young children. She was small and dumpy, and the children had snotty noses and were quite whiny. They ran all over the office touching things. Silently I pitied Jim and congratulated myself for never having gotten married.

Yes, I decided, Jim was the ideal person for my self-exploration. After some checking, I found that he often stayed late on Thursdays. On the very next Thursday, I made it a point to remain at the office after quitting time to finish an account I had been working on. As I reached into the closet for my most flattering low-cut dress, I assured myself that I had no intention of trying to lure Jim away from his wife. I told my guilty conscience that I only wanted to discover how I would react if a man made a play for me now that I had gained insight.

Jim was surprised to see me still at my desk after the others had left.

"We're both workaholics," he remarked, smiling.

I agonized over how to begin. I wished that I had more experience in flirting. With a surge of determination, I turned my chair in his direction. I had an impulse to get up quickly and plop myself down on his lap. I held my breath, started to get up, froze, and had to sit down again.

Time was passing fast. I was afraid that Jim might finish his work and leave. Anxiously, I glanced at him out of the corner of my eye. I was sure he was watching me—just waiting for the slightest encouragement to get up and take me in his arms.

"Jim," I said, feeling my heart beat faster, "I'm glad you're here."

"It's nice to have company when one has to work late," he agreed pleasantly.

I turned my chair a little more so that he could see my crossed legs. My thighs were only partially covered by my short skirt. "I wish I knew what to do with myself tonight," I sighed.

He looked concerned. "You really ought to go out and have more fun, Carol," he said. Jim sounded like an older brother. "An attractive woman like you shouldn't have to be lonely."

Numbly, I watched him gather up the papers on his desk. "I've got to go," he said. "If I get home much later, my wife will complain that work is more important to me than she is." He chuckled at such foolishness. He picked up his briefcase, waved a hand, and was gone.

I was fortunate that the therapist had a cancellation and could see me the next day. I was so low, I felt like I was crawling into her office. I was relieved to see that she wasn't wearing an I-told-you-so look.

With tears flowing, I confessed everything—my not telling her about the flashback of being molested by my grandfather, my futile effort to cure myself, the second flashback of the molestation, and my botched up attempt to use Jim to explore my feelings.

"Your mother called after your last visit," the therapist said after listening to me. "She wanted to be helpful and told me that she has worried about you since you were a child." The therapist paused to check her notes. A moment later she looked up. *"According to your mother, both of your grandfathers died before you were born!"*

I could hardly believe it! Was I crazy? Could all of this have been just my imagination?

"But your mother gave me some additional information that might help explain your memories," the therapist continued. "She told me that when you were a child, you lived with your parents in a large house. Only a part of it was used by your family. Since times were hard, your mother rented out some of the spare rooms. Some roomers were retired men, some were salesmen, and some worked in construction in the industrial park near your home.

"Your father was in college out of town. Your mother worked some evenings as a receptionist at a nearby hotel. On the nights she worked she would sometimes ask one or another of the roomers to keep an eye on you after she put you to bed."

## COMMENT:

*When Carol was a child, one of her friends had a grandfather who entertained them with stories of his adventurous life. Carol didn't have a living grandfather but wanted one of her own, so she created one in her imagination. Children sometimes handle feelings of deprivation in this way.*

*Carol had been sexually molested by the roomers in her parents' house while her mother was working evenings. To avoid the anxiety that recalling these traumatic experiences would bring, Carol repressed her memory of them. However, they lingered in the unconscious part of her mind and were converted into fantasies of a grandfather. Her positive relationships with her father and brother, along with her traumatic experiences with the roomers, later created her "mixed-up" feelings about men.*

*Childhood sexual molestation causes time-spanning scars that usually do not heal without therapeutic intervention. The circumstances and the age of a molested child help shape the personality disorders that may result. These may include social discomfort, difficulty in becoming meaningfully involved with people, self-destroying hypersexuality or, conversely, an abnormal aversion to sex. The time that elapses between any traumatic experience and the beginning of counseling often determines the severity of the disorder that follows.*

*Disorders of this type have been successfully treated by therapists who were able to gain their patients' confidence. A variety of resources exists in the average American community to help families with a child who has been molested. The family doctor is a good source of information and referral. A child should be medically examined as soon as possible after sexual molestation has occurred. Another place to seek help might be state, county, or city-sponsored social services. They can refer families to specialists trained to assist children and adults who have been sexually molested. These agencies often continue to serve the families as a resource of guidance and information.*

*Carol's therapist used the couch in her office for*

*family therapy—not for psychoanalysis. It provided more sitting room for her clients.*

*Tom was glad to see his lawyer come into the room where his claim for a disability pension was going to be heard. With the lawyer's help, the pension he needed to support his family—and to spend his life in leisure—was sure to be awarded to him. Only the psychologist could mess things up. But Tom doubted that he would. His diagnosis, post-traumatic head syndrome manifested by loss of balance and memory difficulty secondary to vasoconstriction, couldn't be ignored by the referee. But one never can be too sure. Life has its strange quirks.*

# TOM:
# Who Is Smarter?

I sat across the desk from the psychologist and eyeballed him. I didn't let his looks scare me.

I warned myself not to be too confident. Skinny guys like him can sometimes surprise you. I remembered getting a black eye from a shrimp his size back in high school. That kid saved himself by being able to run faster than I could. But this time I had to match wits, not muscles, I reminded myself.

I could see the psychologist's certificates on the wall behind him. There was one showing that he had a Ph.D. in psychology and another that he was licensed to practice psychology in the state. A couple more hung on the other walls of his office. I tried not to let them impress me. No matter what this guy asked, I knew that I had to keep my cool like I had the time I saw Dr. Bergson. By remaining alert I came out of that okay.

Bergson was the neurologist who saw me after my accident. I found out (never mind how) that all the tests and scans he gave me came out normal. Nevertheless, the diagnosis I ended up with raised my hopes that I'd get the disability pension I needed to take care of my money problems. I memorized "post traumatic head syndrome manifested by headaches, loss of balance, and memory difficulties, numbness of finger tips possibly secondary to vasoconstriction of brain blood vessels." That's a hefty bunch of words with which to impress the Disability Review Board when it meets in a couple of months.

I watched the psychologist as he leafed through my medical folder. I figured that he had reviewed it before I came in. It was almost an inch thick. Each time a doctor examined me, my folder got a little thicker. Just as I was wondering what the psychologist was thinking, he looked up at me for a moment. Then his eyes returned to the form that I had filled out, describing what had happened to me.

"You were employed by Bidden Brothers, a farm equipment company, for five years prior to your accident. The accident occurred last year on February 2nd. You were working in the field with a cable and a hand winch," he read. "While you were cranking the winch, it broke. A piece of equipment came down and hit you on the right side of your head. Momentarily, you were stunned and lost your speech and movement. In a short time you recovered. Is that right?"

I nodded, "Yes, that's what happened." Was he doubting it? I didn't trust him.

"Later you said that you hadn't passed out, but found you couldn't move your body and you felt weak all over. You said you kept yourself from falling by holding onto the pulley chain. When you went to get help, you noticed that you couldn't walk straight." The psychologist paused and looked at me.

"Yeah," I said, beginning to feel defiant. The psychologist continued reading aloud what I had told the other doctors. "You claim that as a result of the accident, you had difficulty sleeping and lost interest in life. You told one of the doctors that things got so bad that you couldn't even change the oil in your car."

"That's right," I said.

"You are presently taking Motrin and Vicodin for pain, lorazepam to calm you down, and Pamelor to help your depression. That's quite a bit of medication. Do you find that they've helped you?''

Careful boy, I warned myself.

''They do,'' I admitted. ''But I'm not the same guy I was before the accident. I was happy and outgoing and got along with everyone. I slept seven or eight hours every night.''

''And now?'' he asked.

''Now the most I can sleep is four or five hours.''

He read on. ''It says here that after the accident you lost your self-respect and confidence. And even with all the medication you are now taking for anxiety, you still feel depressed and nervous.''

''That's right,'' I told him. ''I feel depressed and nervous. I don't feel like doing anything. I don't feel like talking to anyone or watching TV. I don't even want to do my yard work. The worst thing is what all this has done to my family.'' How could I let that dumbhead know that I wasn't making any of this up!

The psychologist's eyes went back to the folder. ''I see you had physical therapy and biofeedback. Did they help?''

''My headaches got better. I tried to go back to work after my treatments. The first time I went back, I was only able to stay a few hours.

Some kind of fear came over me while I was there. I just couldn't take it. I tried to go back to work again a couple of weeks later after the doctor prescribed more anti-anxiety pills. That time I held out for three weeks doing my regular job with forklifts.''

''And then what happened?'' Was there suspicion in his eyes? For a moment I wondered if he had been paid under-the-table money from Bidden Brothers. Then I figured it was more likely that psychologists were suspicious by nature.

''It felt better to be working than just hanging around,'' I told him, hoping that would impress him. ''I wanted to stay at Bidden Brothers and thought I was doing a good job.''

''Everything seemed to be getting better for me after I returned to my job. But I guess the company didn't think my work was good enough after my injury. They asked me to take a vacation without pay. That was upsetting because I needed to work on account of my financial problems. That's when I went back to see Dr. Dickenson—one of my doctors. I told him I was still afraid of getting hurt. I guess that made me extra careful and slowed me down. Bidden Brothers wasn't satisfied with me because of that.''

''And you've been on medical leave since then?'' the psychologist asked, looking at my folder. I didn't like the way he said it, and felt myself getting angry. It seemed like the son of a bitch didn't believe a thing I said. I tried to make sure that my feelings didn't show on my face. I braced myself for the testing that was coming. I promised myself that no matter what happened, I wouldn't let this guy do me in! I watched him go to a cabinet, pull out some test materials, and place them on his desk.

Now the time has come for me to use my wits, I thought. I took a deep breath. If he wrote "uncooperative" on my chart it would look bad. "Faking" would look worse. I decided the best thing to do was to answer the test questions in a natural way, but keep a sharp lookout for a trap. I was determined not to let the psychological tests beat me into losing my chance for a disability pension. The psychologist, no doubt, was smarter than me, but I had much more to lose. I hoped that this would make me try harder not to let him trap me.

He placed some drawings in front of me and asked me to copy them on a sheet of paper. My strategy was to do it as fast as I could so he couldn't blame me for not being exact.

I also hurried through the long list of questions he asked me to answer. That part was tricky and boring; and I hated it. The questions didn't have anything to do with my accident, and I was afraid that I was being set up. I answered a lot of them with "I don't know." My memory hadn't been good after the accident and "I don't know" fits right into my complaints.

The testing got a bit easier when he handed me some cards with inkblots on them and asked what I could see in them. It didn't seem to me that what I saw or didn't see in the inkblots could tell him anything about my accident. That made me feel safer.

He handed me another bunch of cards with sketches of people doing things. It was one test on which I wasn't going to stick my neck out. I didn't try hard to describe what I thought was going on in the pictures. The danger of being trapped kept me alert. Something told me that the sillier a test looked, the greater chance there was of being trapped.

"Me, draw?" I asked the psychologist when he told me to draw a picture. "I couldn't even draw for my own mother if she held my hand and pushed it around for me!" I told him. As I bent over the paper with pencil in hand I glanced up and it seemed to me that the psychologist was watching me like a hawk. That bothered me. I felt like a sparrow about to become a meal. I quickly drew a few circles for flowers, some wiggly lines for clouds and a big sun. I didn't think it satisfied him because he asked me to draw something else. I drew some scribbles to remind him again that I couldn't draw.

After the testing, the psychologist asked me if I wanted to be trained for a different kind of work—something that would keep me away from machinery. I pretended to think it over. I told him that my headaches would probably keep me from studying. I reminded him of my problem with concentrating. I told him that we were broke, and my family would depend on my disability payments to keep us going. I was glad to see him take notes so that what I had said would be there for the disability board to see when they went over the records. I was pretty sure that I had my disability pension in the bag.

Three months later I found myself nervously sitting in the stuffy, overheated conference room in the courthouse where my hearing was scheduled. I calmed down when the referee representing the State Compensation Board shook my hand and gave me a pleasant smile. He had white hair, a rosy complexion, and looked like someone's kindly grandfather. Lucky, I told myself, to get a nice guy like him to be the referee instead of some strict, sour-faced guy.

I was glad to see my lawyer come in carrying a briefcase. I knew that he was sharp and would fight hard for my disability pension.

The referee had my thick folder in front of

him. I figured he must have spent a lot of time going through it because he seemed to be able to find everything he was looking for quickly.

"I have read about your injury and the reports of your doctors. Do you think you are able to go back to work?" he asked me straight off.

"I don't know," I said. "I sure would like to, Sir."

The referee turned some pages in my folder.

My lawyer broke in with, "He tried twice to do that. The first time on. . . ."

"Yes, I know," the referee said, stopping him. "I have all that right in front of me." Turning to me he asked, "What would happen if you went back to work now?"

"Well" I said, grateful for my lawyer's lead-in, "I'm afraid the same thing would happen that happened before."

"And that was?"

Why was he asking me this? He had it all in front of him. Was he trying to trip me up?

"Well, I'm no longer as good or as fast at work as I used to be. My boss would see that and probably let me go."

"You wouldn't be as good at work again as you were before the accident? And why is that?"

"I guess my fear of getting hurt again would

slow me up," I explained thinking he was tougher than I had expected. "The kind of work I did at Bidden Brothers doesn't allow me to slow up."

"And how do you feel about being retrained for a different kind of work?"

I shot a glance at my lawyer and immediately realized that looking at him was a mistake. The old guy saw it.

"I'd like that," I said pretending to think it over. "But my nerves aren't as good as they were before the accident," I added.

My lawyer turned to the referee. "May I ask my client how the medications prescribed for him by his physicians are affecting him?"

The referee signaled for me to speak. "Well," I said, choosing my words carefully, "they're making me tired. I find that I can't concentrate."

"I have called in an expert witness," the referee said as the psychologist strode in and took a seat at the table. I felt my muscles tighten.

The referee didn't waste much time. Pointing at me, he asked the psychologist, "Do you know this person?"

"Yes, Sir," the psychologist said, looking at me. "I did a psychological evaluation."

"And what were your findings?"

"There was no indication of neurological impairment on the testing and no signs of psychosis. Instead, the testing reflected anxiety and some depression. His performance suggested that he was evasive. In my opinion there was some malingering."

"The son of a bitch!" I muttered under my breath.

"Does your evaluation suggest that the claimant is capable of going back to work?"

"Yes. I think that he can go back to work and do what he did before. He does not require vocational rehabilitation. Perhaps, the medications he is taking are causing some of his present problems."

"Do you have a medical degree?" my lawyer shot at him.

"I have a Ph.D. in psychology, clinical internship, and. . . ."

The referee interrupted, raising his hand. "No need to go into that. You were appointed by the review board as fully qualified to make the evaluation."

That was it. The referee dismissed us, stating that he would make his recommendations to the review board. Turning to me he said that I would hear the board's decision in about sixty days.

Almost exactly two months later I got the

news that the board had decided I was able to go back to work. The next day I returned to my former job at Bidden Brothers. Before long, I found myself working even harder than I had before the accident. The bosses recognized it and showed their appreciation by giving me a pretty good raise.

After a while, I was glad I hadn't gotten the pension. I know that if I had, I'd just be hanging around the house, depressed and having symptoms. I'd be taking pills, getting in my wife's way, and probably be setting a poor example for the kids. Working hard actually made me feel healthier than I ever had before. My family life was great now. It seems the psychologist had really done me a favor. Life has its strange quirks, I thought as I looked back on my hearing a year later.

Yes, life has its strange quirks, I thought again six months after that as I reread the letter which informed me that the appeal submitted by the lawyer had been successful. The review board had reconsidered its decision and my disability pension had belatedly been approved with payments dating back to the time of my injury.

## COMMENT:

*The idea of malingering occurred to Tom after he had been seen by various physicians who gave him prognoses he felt were vague and disturbing. His intention to malinger crystallized shortly before his mandatory visit to the psychologist.*

*After Tom made the decision to try for a disability pension, he exaggerated the symptoms he had and faked others. Later, he half believed that his exaggerated and faked symptoms were real. Fact and fiction became entangled in his mind.*

*Tom's easily aroused anxiety was a personality characteristic that he'd had long before his accident. His anxiety gave credence to his statement that he had a fear of getting hurt again on the job. It wasn't hard for Tom to convince himself that he was entitled to a disability pension that would help solve his financial problems. But he believed that if he didn't watch his step, the psychologist would cheat him out of what in his mind had become his "right."*

*Tom was unaware that he had demonstrated malingering and "test resistance" during his psychological evaluation. He saw the psychologist as an adversary whose aim was to deprive him of this chance to get a disability pension. Tom felt self-righteous, but we can assume that he could not blot out his awareness that he was inflating his reports of discomfort and exaggerating his symptoms. This provided Tom with a challenge. "Who is smarter?"*

*he asked himself as he attempted to outwit the psychologist.*

*Generalizations about claimants attempting to obtain disability pensions should not be made by what has been reported in this narrative. Most disability awards are deserved. But Tom was right—''Life has its quirks!''*

*Freddy knew that fire is a no-no. But when he found the candles burning on his birthday cake the year he turned nineteen, he decided that little fires on a birthday cake are okay. "You're a good boy," the man at the store told him. Still Freddy worried about what his father had said. "If you're a bad boy, you'll be sent away," he had warned him. And Freddy remembered it always.*

# FREDDY:
# There's No Place Like Home

Sarah and I celebrated Freddy's first birthday with a small cake. We hid our tears behind smiles as we raised our glasses and drank to our son's health.

Our pediatrician had told us a few months after Freddy's birth that our baby was what he called "developmentally delayed." In a kind way, he informed us it was unlikely that Freddy would ever grow up to become a normal adult. We had feared this ever since Freddy was just three or four months old. He didn't seem as responsive as other babies and didn't do many of the things other babies his age did. Even at six months, he couldn't turn over by himself.

When he was a year old, he still wasn't imitating sounds and was just barely beginning to crawl.

"Oh, he'll catch up," we told each other, not quite believing it. Our pediatrician examined him thoroughly and gave him numerous tests. He wasn't as optimistic as we pretended we were. As each month passed and we failed to see any real progress in Freddy's development, we tried to resign ourselves to having a child who would never be normal. Nevertheless, I was unable to stamp out of my mind the hope that a new drug would be found or a miracle would occur which would make Freddy like other children.

Sarah's pregnancy had been uneventful and she was healthy throughout. We had no relatives who were mentally impaired. Our physician told us that Freddy's condition was probably caused by a problem that had occurred early in his embryonic development. He explained that the cause is not clearly understood and assured us that we were in no way responsible. Knowing that we were not to blame helped us to make peace with the idea that our son might remain a child mentally throughout his entire life.

When Freddy was three years old, our pediatrician recommended that we take him to a psychologist who specialized in evaluating young children. Sarah and I promised ourselves that we would be courageous if the results of the examination confirmed our fears.

We sat in the psychologist's waiting room, holding hands, while Freddy was evaluated. After about an hour and a half, the psychologist came into the waiting room leading Freddy by the hand. He told us that Freddy has been restless but quite cooperative throughout the examination. As he shook our hands and patted Freddy on the head, he informed us that he would send his report to our pediatrician and told us to make an appointment with him to discuss the results.

It upset Sarah to have to wait for the results. "Why couldn't he have told us himself what he found out?" she complained as we left. "A psychologist should know how hard it is for parents to wait to learn what is wrong with their child!"

"They've got their rules," I tried to assure her. I hoped that the psychological evaluation would show that Freddy could benefit from some kind of training which would bring his development closer to normal. Surely there was something we could do, I thought.

The next week was really difficult. While we waited for the appointment with the pediatrician, we tried to convince ourselves that, with a lot of help from us, Freddy would become more like a normal child. We were wrong.

"I've read over the psychologist's evaluation," the pediatrician began. "Freddy seems to have a broad range of developmental deficits. His psychomotor impairment and the level of his performance skills place him in the top range of the Severe Mental Retardation category. Of course, we suspected that, didn't we?" he asked us as he glanced at our serious faces.

"The psychologist notes that Freddy is a pleasant child who is more cooperative than many other children with the same amount of impairment, and that is good news."

"What will he be able to do when he grows up?" Sarah asked anxiously.

"At Freddy's age things are still fluid, so we can't make exact predictions," the doctor replied. "Children with Freddy's degree of retardation can be trained in hygiene skills. They can learn to do some counting, and occasionally, even a limited amount of reading. As an adult, Freddy will probably be able to maintain a conversation at the level of a four- or five-year-old child. He is less likely than some children with similar defects to exhibit socially disruptive behavior when he grows up. But, as I said, he is too young for us to make many predictions. Freddy must be re-evaluated periodically in order to obtain a developmental profile over time."

"My recommendation would be that you contact Social Services," he continued. "They have many programs which will help to maximize his potential. Some of these are residential and others are day-school situations. A social worker can assist you in making some important decisions."

Sarah was doing her best to hold back tears, but I could see her expression harden as the doctor continued talking.

"You could try to keep him at home and enroll him in a specialized day school," he suggested. "Truthfully, more might be done for Freddy if he were placed in a residential home where a full-time professional staff could devote time and attention to him. There, they would be able to observe him and use special education and conditioning techniques to increase Freddy's coping skills."

As soon as we got to Sarah's sister's house, where we had left Freddy while we were at the pediatrician's, my wife ran to him, picked him up and said to me, "I couldn't love him more if he were an Einstein! I'll keep him at home with me as long as I live!" Then, as if he could understand, she said to Freddy, "Don't you worry, dear. You'll never be sent away from home."

For weeks after that, I kept thinking of the problems that lay ahead. I felt that I could love

Freddy just as much if we had to visit him in a residential facility. I believed that if it were to his advantage, we'd be showing him greater love by placing him there. Certainly, it would be easier for all of us if Freddy didn't live at home. I knew Sarah felt differently. She would keep Freddy at home no matter how difficult it might prove to be.

I must admit that Freddy remained affectionate and docile. Still, as he grew older, he became more difficult to handle. But Sarah continued to devote herself to him. She spent her afternoons and many evenings working with him on the developmental tasks his teacher at Mrs. Mary's Day School for Exceptional Children recommended.

After a while, it occurred to me that Sarah might be more willing to consider placing Freddy in a residential facility if we were to have another child. I longed for a normal child who might make our family life more wholesome and happier than it had become. I knew that Sarah also wanted another child. Naturally, we had some fear that the second child might also be mentally defective in some way. But when our second son, Robert, was born, there wasn't a moment of doubt about his development. Our joy was great. Sarah was radiant. Yet, I still felt that she loved Freddy more than the new baby.

Although Freddy was intrigued by his baby brother and was affectionate toward him, things got more complicated as Robert grew older and began to assert himself. Freddy didn't understand that he was bigger and stronger than Robert. Several times, when both boys were reaching for the same toy, I saw Freddy push Robert roughly. It was after one of those times that I took Freddy aside. Making sure that Sarah was not within earshot, I told him sternly, "Freddy, you must never hit or push anyone." I gently demonstrated hitting and pushing. "If you ever do that again, you will not be allowed to live here at home. You will be a bad boy and bad boys must be sent away. Do you hear what I am telling you?"

Freddy looked serious. I felt he got the message, but couldn't be sure he would remember my warning for more than an hour—a day or two at most.

"Tell me what I said!" I commanded.

"Hitting is a no-no," he replied solemnly, his head bowed.

It was about that time that Freddy really gave us a scare. He found a box of matches in the kitchen. He lit one and held it to a roll of paper towels. Fortunately, Sarah walked into the room before the burning paper did any damage. I was reading in the living room when I heard her scream, "No! No! Bad boy!" I got to the kitchen just in time to see her emphasizing her words with some swats on Freddy's bottom.

The years passed quickly. When Freddy was fourteen years old we welcomed the birth of our daughter, Betty. I hoped that our love for our new little daughter would bring Sarah and me closer together, as we had been before Freddy was born.

I had no complaints about Freddy's behavior toward his little sister. From the start he was caring and curious. Although he remained gentle, I was more than half convinced that some day he would prove dangerous to her because he was not aware of his own strength. I was afraid he might hurt Betty if she did something to anger him and we were not there to protect her. I no longer worried that he would hurt Robert, because by this time Robert could hold his own with Freddy.

Regardless of what he did, Sarah was Freddy's advocate, usually excusing his actions with ''He didn't mean it.'' We began to have frequent quarrels about the children, and our marriage started to slide downhill. Gradually, I spent more time with the bottle than with my wife. ''Am I becoming an alcoholic?'' I asked myself. When I had to answer, ''probably,'' I started worrying about myself. It even occurred to me that it would be wise for me to get some professional help before it was too late. But I felt that without drinking I could no longer tolerate Sarah's obsessive devotion to Freddy. She loves him a lot more than she loves me, I thought, feeling bitter.

One evening, while thinking of how discontented I had become with my life, I suddenly recalled reading that retarded children do not have a full life span. The article said that most die before they reach their teens, and relatively few severely retarded children survive more than twenty years. At the time I read it, the impact this could have on us didn't fully register in my mind. I wasn't entirely sober on that particular evening when I pictured myself, with a secret sense of relief, comforting Sarah at Freddy's funeral. "You knew, of course, that retarded children die early," I imagined myself telling her. Then, in my daydream, I saw myself living in a cozy home with a loving wife and two normal children. I had my arm around my wife and was looking forward to again enjoying a love life.

When I returned to reality, I sighed and felt guilty. Some things are probably too good to be true, I thought.


FREDDY:

I see little lights on the cake. Mamma and Daddy say, "Happy Birthday, Freddy. You're nineteen years old today!"

I say, "That's old! Fire is a no-no, but little fires on a birthday cake are good. I like cake. I like birthdays."

"Happy Birthday, Freddy," my sister, Betty, says and gives me a kiss. "Happy Birthday," my aunt says. Robert is there, too. Then everyone sings "Happy Birthday, Freddy."

Later, Mamma takes me to Mrs. Mary's School. There I put the ball in the box. I put the lid on the box. I turn the box the way the teacher did. I shake the box like the teacher did. I take the lid off. I take the ball out. The teacher claps her hands. I clap my hands. I feel good. Some other boys at school push me and laugh. I don't hit them. Hitting is a no-no. Daddy said if I hit, I am a bad boy. If I am a bad boy I will have to go away. I don't want to leave home. I don't want to leave Mamma and Daddy and Betty.

I help Mamma. I am strong and can carry things. When Mamma writes down on paper what she wants from the store, I walk to the store with the paper. I talk to nobody but the man in the store. I show him the paper and he gets all the things Mamma wants and puts them in a bag for me to carry home.

Today, Mamma says, "I'm tired." Daddy is thirsty. He keeps drinking brown water. He is laughing and singing. Betty is crying. Robert is there, too.

Mamma says, "Here's a list of things I want you to bring back from the store. Hurry! Daddy needs to eat right away!"

When I got to the store, the man said, "Hi, Freddy. Give me that paper." Then he says, "Come into the back of the store and help me lift some boxes." I lift the boxes. They are very heavy.

The man says, "You are a good boy, Freddy, and you're no problem. You have a wonderful family. Few parents would do what they are doing for you." He puts his hand on my shoulder. "Now, you wait here while I get the things your mother wants."

He gives me the bag filled with the food Mamma wants for Daddy and I start to go home. Outside there are loud noises. The man stops and listens. He says, "Hear those sirens, Freddy? There must be a fire somewhere nearby."

I remember that I have to hurry and start walking home fast. Soon I see my house. Fire trucks are out there. I smell smoke that hurts my eyes. I see fire coming out of my house. Parts of the house are on the sidewalk. Smoke is coming from the pieces. A policeman stops me from going into my house. I tell him, "Mamma wants the things I got at the store. She said Daddy needs to eat right away."

The policeman keeps pushing me back. I tell

him, "Mamma and Daddy said that fire is a no-no." I ask him, "Why is there fire in our house?"

I see more smoke coming out of our house. Lots of people are on the street watching. Red lights are going off and on. Firemen are running around our house. A big white car is coming. Men with white coats get out of it and run toward our house. Some policemen come over to me and want me to go with them. I don't want to. I want to give Mamma the food for Daddy. I want to go into my house. They won't let me. I don't like the policemen.

NEWSPAPER ITEM:

Fire, caused by the explosion of a faulty gas heater, burned out of control in a home here yesterday. A mentally defective young man, who was out of the house at the time of the fire, is the sole survivor of a family of five. The young man struggled with police and tried to enter the burning building. He said he had to give the groceries he was carrying to his mother because his father was hungry.

The young man was taken to the State Hospital for the Severely Retarded. On his arrival at the facility, he was crying and said, "I didn't give Mamma the food from the store. I am a bad boy. Now Daddy won't let me live at home anymore."

## COMMENT:

*Mental retardation, or developmental delay as it is frequently referred to, falls into the mental health category of Developmental Disorders. Some of these are associated with a genetic defect or with specific conditions such as Down's Syndrome or Fetal Alcohol Syndrome. Freddy's handicap may have resulted from abnormal reproduction of chromosomes. More frequently developmental disorders occur as a result of toxins, infections, or maternal consumption of alcohol—all of which interfere with normal development of the foetus.*

*About four percent of mentally retarded persons fall into the Severe Mental Retardation category. They may do well in group homes and, if they have no severe behavioral difficulties, some of them may remain in their own homes, if supervision is available.*

*The presence of a retarded child may give rise to conflicts of the kind that occurred in Freddy's home. If there are other children in the home, pronounced sibling rivalries may develop. Sometimes one of the parents may be jealous of the amount of time and attention the other parent pays to the retarded child. In some cases, deeply buried death wishes for the handicapped child may surface—usually during therapy—and these wishes are almost always accompanied by guilt. In most communities, there are family counseling and support groups available to help a family cope with such problems. Most public*

and private social work agencies have qualified
workers ready to assist families adjust to having and
caring for a developmentally delayed child.

Whereas the strain of keeping a severely mentally
retarded person at home may be considerable, it is
the complex emotional conflicts that often accompany doing so that tend to cause the most disruption.
But here, as elsewhere, "Man proposes—God dis-
poses" holds. Freddy could not have understood
this. His mom and dad did not live long enough to
find out how it applied to their separate and very
different hopes for Freddy.

*It was an unusual assignment, but a clever one.
The residents of an alcoholic treatment center were
asked to present their life histories centered around
a person who had been very influential in their lives.
Tommy chose his sister, Elizabeth. This, too, was
unusual since the others chose parents or mates. He
couldn't help Elizabeth when he discovered that she
had become an alcoholic. He could only condemn
her even as he, himself, fell victim to the same
malady.*

# TOMMY and ELIZABETH:
# Role Model

My name is Tommy. I'm a resident in a large
West Coast alcoholic treatment center. All of
us in my therapy group are older residents—let
us say "more mature" instead of "older." We
were asked by our group leader to write about
a lifelong association we've had with a person
or persons who were influential in our lives.

The eight people in my group therapy section
had become alcoholics later in life than most of
the other residents at the center. We were asked
to describe the beginning of the relationship and
include sufficient details to make our presentation useful as a topic for discussion at a later
meeting.

So far, three residents had read their stories and we had interesting, lively discussions and sometimes arguments about the roles played by the persons who were described. One described a relationship with parents, another with a husband, and the third with a live-in girlfriend. I viewed my older sister, Elizabeth, as the one who best fitted the description as the most influential person in my life.

The group meeting had begun. It was my turn to read my story: "I'm married but it was my older sister, Elizabeth, who had always had a great influence on my life before I came to the center. Her husband died in a car accident several months after she was married and she never remarried. After that she may have thought of me as the child she had wanted but never had. To this day she refers to me as 'Tommy, my baby brother.'

"While we lived in the same city it was easy for me and Elizabeth to visit back and forth. But six years ago Elaine, my wife, and I moved across the country to the West Coast. Elizabeth remained in New York. I tried to keep in touch with her and for a while we managed pretty well by weekly telephone calls and occasional flights to New York. It was always a joyous reunion when I visited her in the West Side apartment where she lived after her retirement from the advertising agency where she had been employed as a commercial artist.

"Some time after we had moved West, we received a phone call from the seventy-year-old woman who shared Elizabeth's apartment. She told us that Elizabeth had had a bad fall and had been taken to the hospital. I called the hospital and was told that Elizabeth had broken her hip, and had been very drunk when she was admitted.

"For a number of years I had had a strong suspicion that Elizabeth was drinking far too much. Whenever I asked her about this, she always denied it. More ominous, on one of my visits I found that she had hidden some bottles of brandy in various closets. Some of her friends confirmed my fear that Elizabeth had become an alcoholic.

"During my last visit to New York, I remained a week longer than I had planned to stay. I spent the time trying to convince Elizabeth to get treatment for her alcohol addiction. I contacted a psychiatrist who headed an alcohol rehabilitation program in a large New York hospital. After insisting that alcohol was not a problem and that she didn't need help, she at last agreed to see him. She turned up sober for her interview and was clever enough to convince him that she was not an alcoholic. Knowing that she hid bottles of brandy throughout the apartment and compulsively drank throughout much of the day and night, I was stunned to find that she had been able to outwit a specialist in alcohol abuse.

"Elizabeth's addiction occurred gradually. She became aware that she was experiencing difficulty in hearing what people at her office were saying. She knew our mother had become deaf as she grew older and had always feared that this might happen to her, too. Elizabeth never had been a very patient person. After experimenting with hearing aids, Elizabeth stubbornly decided that they were uncomfortable and did not help her enough to put up with them. In time, Elizabeth's hearing loss became more severe and she was no longer able to interact with people easily. She was involuntarily retired from her job at the advertising agency. Many of her friends drifted away and she began to turn inward. Apparently, she tried to escape from isolation by consuming ever-increasing amounts of brandy.

"While Elizabeth was hospitalized, I learned that she suffered from occasional seizures and had developed a chronic loss of memory. Upon her discharge from the hospital after her hip had healed, Elizabeth experienced difficulty in walking. It became impossible for her to continue living in her apartment and, finally, we had to place her in a nursing home in New York City. It was the city she had once told me she would never leave.

"After she had been at the nursing home for several months, I received a letter from the social worker there stating that attempts to rehabilitate Elizabeth's hip had been unsuccessful and that she was permanently wheelchair-bound. On receiving this discouraging news, I flew to New York to visit her.

"Elizabeth's room was on the fifth floor of a huge drab-looking building. As the elevator door opened at her floor, I caught a glimpse of Elizabeth sitting expressionless in a wheelchair in the hallway. I walked toward her and saw that her teeth were stained almost black. I later learned that it was caused by the iron supplement she was given for her alcohol-related anemia. Her eyes were vacant, but her face was as unlined and her skin still as beautiful and clear as it had always been.

"Standing in front of her wheelchair so that she could see me, I called her name. 'Elizabeth,' I repeated, moving closer. Her head lifted. She stared at me for a moment and turned away, not recognizing me.

" 'Elizabeth, I am your brother, Tommy. Your baby brother,' I said, speaking so loud that I was almost shouting. After a few moments I saw recognition dawn in her eyes. Slowly her hand reached out toward me.

" 'I know you. Of course I know you!' she

said in a voice stronger than I had anticipated. 'You are my baby brother, Tommy.'

"Elizabeth seemed to become more oriented each day I visited her. She told me that she had been lonely and had missed me. It was then that I decided to move her to a nursing home out West near our home. I was certain that living in New York City had, by this time, little meaning to her.

"In spite of warnings about the difficulty of transferring elderly persons from one nursing home to another, we had no problem in flying her across the country. The agency that handled her transfer was experienced and efficient. Elizabeth adjusted quickly to the change of nursing homes and seemed to respond to my frequent visits with a renewed will to live. 'I love you, Tommy,' she would say when she saw me. 'You are so loyal to me.' Then, her eyes would turn toward a severely disabled occupant of an adjacent wheelchair. 'I hope that coming here doesn't depress you.'

" 'No, Elizabeth,' I tried to reassure her. 'When I am here with you I don't feel depressed.' It was true. I would not have anticipated that I could relax among people who are wheelchair-bound. In the nursing home with my sister I was able to escape from phone calls, mail, bills, and making appointments. Nowhere else, except when I sat next to my sister in the empty room where I usually wheeled her, was I able to stop worrying about the increasing difficulty I had in coping at work and with the problems I had in my marriage. In the nursing home, a place many people equate with living hell, I found precious moments of peace.

"But not in the halls where a circle of wheelchairs ringed the nurses' station. There I couldn't shut out the intermittent cries of 'Help me!' from people who had deteriorated far beyond any possibility of help. I could not avoid noticing the empty husks in human shape, some with eyes staring, fingers twitching, saliva drooling down their chins. I realized then that far worse than dying, for those who are suffering and beyond recovery, is wanting to die and not being able to. A shrill, persistent beeping at the nurses' station cut through all other sounds. I found, as time went on, my initial revulsion was replaced by a thought that was strange and frightening—here with Elizabeth is where I really belong.

"For years I had been worrying about my increasing difficulty in concentrating and my frequent headaches. I began to realize that I had occasional dizzy spells and, at times, even difficulty in keeping my balance. You all know what was happening to me but I refused to see it. I told myself that by visiting the nursing home so frequently, I had somehow adopted some of the symptoms of the residents. It was a foolish idea and, of course, I really knew better. You all know how determined we alcoholics are to use denial. I used it almost to the day I entered the treatment center.

"My wife, Elaine, told me several times that it would make sense for me to go for counseling, but I refused. I insisted that it wasn't necessary, just as Elizabeth had earlier. I always looked forward to visiting my sister and felt secure in her presence and safe in the nursing home's restricted environment.

"But that changed one day when I stopped in to see Elizabeth early in the morning. She seemed to be asleep when I first entered her room, but a few minutes later, while I was at her bedside, her body shook and she began to sob rhythmically. Alarmed, I pressed the call button at Elizabeth's bed. When the nurse arrived, the spasms had been replaced by a twitching of Elizabeth's cheek and mouth.

"For several days after the seizure, Elizabeth was confused and disoriented. She thought she was back in the nursing home in New York and asked to see people who had taken care of her there. Then she insisted that she had to return to her New York apartment, becoming alarmed when she thought that she had failed to lock the apartment door. She was concerned that our parents, long dead, were waiting for her outside in the lobby of the nursing home. It was shocking to see the different person she had suddenly become. It hurt me very much to find that she now hardly recognized me.

"It was then that the anger—no, the rage—I had been holding back for so long, hit me with full force. I found myself condemning my sister for her stupidity in ruining her body and her mind with alcohol! Even now, after all the years, it still seemed unreal to me. Unspoken words went through my mind. 'Elizabeth, what have you done to yourself, you fool!' I felt my eyes filling with tears. 'You once were my role model!'

"I imagined my parents agonizing over my sister. How fortunate it was that they were dead, spared from witnessing their daughter's self-destruction. As I left that day, I whispered, 'I hate you, Elizabeth, for what you have done to yourself.'

"I approached the entrance of the nursing home the following day expecting that Elizabeth would be agitated and deluded.

" 'You've come, Tommy,' Elizabeth said pleasantly, recognizing me the minute she saw me. I bent over and kissed her forehead. 'Tommy,' she said looking up at me lovingly, 'you are so loyal. It makes my life worth living to see you. You are my baby brother.'

"That evening Elaine left home to play her

weekly bridge game with the girls. I pushed the drapes aside just enough to make sure her car had pulled out of the driveway. I started to rush to the closet where I kept my work clothes, but found that walking fast made me lose my balance. Behind some boots I seldom wore, was my current bottle of brandy. I was sure that Elaine would not look for it there. I gloated that, over the years, Elaine had seldom caught me with a bottle in my hand. When she did, I had always been able to talk her out of her suspicions.

"The bottle in the closet was almost empty, but I knew that there were other bottles in other hiding places. I had forgotten exactly where I had put some of them. My memory wasn't as good as it used to be. But it'll be better when I grow up, I thought vaguely as I said aloud, 'Elizabeth, I am your baby brother.' Soon after that I came here to the treatment center."

"That's my story." I looked around at the eight faces that were turned in my direction. From their expressions I could not decide what they thought of my presentation. "We shall discuss it at the next session," the group leader announced. Had I fulfilled the requirement, I wondered.

## COMMENT:

*Tommy had fulfilled his requirement, the members of the therapy group agreed at the next session. The discussion that followed was lively. Before the group was satisfied, Tommy had to explain that he did not blame Elizabeth for his own alcoholism. He acknowledged that even without an alcoholic sister as a role model he would have been prone to alcoholism in view of his life-style and loss of values. His narrative led other members of the group to talk about how they, also, had used denial throughout most of their lives.*

*Alcoholism has among its victims people who experience stress, loneliness, social isolation, physical pain or loss of a physical function such as hearing. A genetic predisposition to alcoholism has been proposed and debated.*

*Elizabeth had secretly been an alcoholic many years and, in time, she succumbed to Korsakoff's syndrome. Patients with this condition retain memory of old events but cannot recall recent events or learn new skills. The condition may occur after prolonged and heavy drinking of alcohol and is usually accompanied by severe vitamin deficiency. Periodically, there may be atypical seizures followed by confusion, loss of awareness, and hallucinations. It is interesting that despite disorientation and memory loss, there may be little apparent intellectual loss. It is this retention of intellectual abilities and* old memories that may confuse relatives of patients who have Korsakoff's syndrome.

Others in Tommy's group wanted to know how Elizabeth had been able to ''outwit'' the psychiatrist Tommy had sent her to see. Many alcoholics are remarkably clever in hiding their alcohol abuse from those who wish to help them, and that even includes professionals in the substance-abuse field. Tommy, like Elizabeth, was successful in blocking awareness of his alcohol addiction out of his mind. Acceptance of the fact that one is an alcoholic is the first essential step in any program of rehabilitation.

*Before Jim could stop her, Andy's wife picked up his blue canvas bag and led him to the guest room. He saw her look of surprise when she found how heavy the bag was. He hoped that she would never guess what was in it. The very next day, eleven innocent people learned his secret—but they didn't live long enough to talk about it.*

*. Jim's story is not an account of events that actually occurred, but a psychological reconstruction of circumstances that could lead to the scenario described.*

# JIM:
# They Weren't Strangers

Yesterday they told me I didn't get the construction job I had applied for at Sam Petinato's. "Sorry, Jim," they said. "Check back in a couple of months. Something may turn up then." To me it sounded like the standard brush-off. My shoulders aren't as broad as some of the guys working there.

Since I left home three years ago, I've been fired from more jobs than I can count. Each time it happens, I hear my dad saying, "There goes that no-good son of mine, goofing up again just as I expected."

Back home Dad used to make fun of the way

I talked when I was little. I couldn't get words to come out of my mouth right. Mom loved my smarter brothers, Andy and George, more than she loved me, and she made no bones about it. My brothers laughed when Dad called me lazy and stupid. One thing Dad didn't know was that I never paid attention to what he said. Talk don't hurt me. Touch me and that's another thing. I never could stand anyone touching me.

After I left home I kept myself going by washing dishes, sweeping floors, working a few days with clean-up crews at construction sites, and doing odd jobs wherever I could find them. A gang of guys that hung around the railway station, where I often slept, used to empty my pockets whenever they could catch me. When they couldn't find any money, they'd beat me up.

One night after they gave me a swollen lip and a bloody nose, I broke into an old house not far from the station. There wasn't much traffic on the street and some of the street lights were out. I hid behind a hedge and looked the house over. I didn't see any lights in the windows. Nothing moved behind the mostly torn drapes. I crept up to the house and found a window that was unlocked. I opened it and pulled myself in. The house smelled musty.

By the light of the matches I lit I could see

clothes scattered around on chairs and an un-made bed. There was a dresser which had some photos of people on it. Lighting more matches, I opened one of the dresser drawers and found old socks, dirty shorts, a couple of extension cords, and some other odds and ends, including a cigarette lighter. I used the lighter to get a better look at the room. Except for a couple of broken chairs, there wasn't much there.

Using the lighter, I looked around in a few more rooms and found them empty. It seemed like a guy must have lived in just that one room. In the kitchen, there were some empty cans and dirty dishes. I didn't waste much time in there. I headed back out, thinking that I couldn't have picked a crummier place to rob. I don't know what made me look under the bed just before I got to the open window to leave.

There was a lot of dust under the bed. Streaks of it were pushed aside by someone who had shoved a magazine under there. I opened it and found pictures of naked women in various sexy poses. I looked further under the bed. I couldn't believe my luck! Beyond the magazine which had partly covered it, I saw a mean-looking snub-nosed assault pistol. It was loaded with shells lining its curved clip. I pulled it out care-fully and found out it was very heavy. Just hold-ing the gun in my hand gave me a feeling of power I'd never had before. I made up my mind right then and there that the gun and I would never part.

I took the gun and decided I'd better get out of there fast. But before I got to the window, I turned back to the photos on the dresser. There was one of a man and woman, both smiling. There was another one of three little kids standing in a row and one of a guy in a uniform. I wondered why they had been left behind by someone who had once lived in the house. I ripped up the pictures and let the pieces fall to the floor. Holding the gun tightly, I walked to the window and crawled out. I hid the gun in the waist of my pants and pulled out my torn shirt to cover it.

A couple of weeks later, I got one of the biggest surprises of my life. I was sitting in a park where a lot of guys who weren't working hung out. I was luckier than most of them because I had been working with a landscape crew for the last couple of weeks and had even rented a room at an old boarding house in the area. I was sitting by myself, biting off hunks of bread and stuffing cold cuts into my mouth, when a guy I had seen looking around walked over to me. He looked familiar, but at first, I couldn't quite place him. Then it hit me that it was my brother, Andy. He recognized me right away.

"Hi, Jim," Andy said and stopped. He looked me over. "You haven't changed all that much, except you're thinner. But then you always were skinny,'' he added, shrugging. His glance took in my stained jeans and torn T-shirt.

''The company I work for asked me to look for some old houses in this town,'' Andy said. ''The company buys old houses and tears them down to build apartments. I was looking at an old boardinghouse and told the lady with dyed red hair who ran it that my name was Burkhard. She told me that a guy with the same name rented a room in her house. She said his first name was Jim.

''When I told her that he might be my brother, she laughed as if I were making a joke. But when I described you, she said I might find you here in the park. So, how are you? How are things going, Jim?''

''Fine,'' I said, grinning. I offered him what was left of my bread and meat. ''Have lunch with me,'' I invited. I laughed when I saw a look of distaste cross his face. He shook his head. ''I'm not hungry,'' he explained.

''Mother has been looking for you,'' Andy went on. ''She wants to see you. She told me that if I ever run into you I should tell you to come home. Dad wants to see you, too. He said that he wants to make up with you for things that happened in the past. Why don't you pack your things at the boardinghouse and come home with me . . . for a visit.''

"No, thanks," I said, smiling at him.

"Okay," Andy said, "But I ought to tell you that Dad hasn't got much longer to live. He's got cancer from all those years of chain smoking. The doctor said he hasn't more than a month or so. He's been operated on twice, but the cancer has been out of control for six months."

"Is he in the hospital?" I asked.

"No, he's home. He wants to die at home. He says he wants to see you before he dies. Why don't you give him that one break? You'll never have a second chance. It's now or never."

Like in a dream I saw myself again as a small child. I recalled my father throwing me a big ball. We tossed it back and forth for a while. I remembered him clapping when I caught it. When it slid through my arms and rolled on the floor he said, "You made a good try, son."

My mind seemed to take me back to another world. I could recall Dad trying to teach me to pronounce words correctly when I got them mixed up. I was surprised that I could now remember him telling Mom not to worry about my not speaking right. "He'll grow out of it in time," he reassured her. My mind took me back even further. I remembered crying after falling down. I must have been no more than a couple of years old. Dad picked me up and gave me a ride on his shoulders.

"I'll go home with you, Andy," I told him. "I'll see Dad."

"Good," Andy said. "Do you need to go back to your room before we head off?"

I nodded. I wanted to get my blue canvas bag which I had hidden under some old newspapers in the bottom of the closet in my room at the boardinghouse.

"Then let's get it and get moving," Andy said, starting away. "My car is over there." He pointed to a blue Mercedes parked at the curb. "Dad, Mom, and George sure will be glad to see you!"

The ride home was smooth. The car had a leather and new-car smell, but my mind wasn't taking this in. I was in a daze, not quite able to think, and only half aware of what was happening. I kept saying to myself, "I'm going home," and then a scary feeling would come over me. I wondered what kind of greeting Mom would give me. Would she hug me when I got there?

Andy tried to ask me questions about my life during the years I had been away, but I pretended I was dozing and didn't hear him. After a while we drove in silence.

It seemed like a long three-hour ride before things started to look familiar. When we got close to the house, I remembered the turn off the freeway. We passed the school we had gone to as kids. Andy and George had been honor students and on the baseball team, while I stayed to myself, hating every minute of it. Andy drove to the section of town where the rich people lived. We stopped at a big house with lots of shrubbery and trees.

Two small kids, a boy and a girl, came running as the Mercedes pulled into the driveway. ''Daddy is here,'' they sang and did a little dance. Pretty soon a good-looking woman joined them and gave Andy a big hug.

''Was it a hard ride home, Andy?'' she asked, stopping short when she caught sight of me. The kids stared at me, too.

''This is your Uncle Jim,'' Andy told them. ''He's been living upstate and came for a visit. Say 'Hello, Uncle Jim,' '' he instructed the kids. They kept on looking at me without saying a word.

''Peggy, this is my brother, Jim,'' Andy announced, turning to his wife. ''I picked him up right at his construction job—didn't even give him time to go home and change.'' It didn't surprise me that he was ashamed of how I was dressed.

''Well, Jim,'' Peggy responded, taking in my dirty jeans and torn shirt, but pretending not to, ''you must have been in a hurry to come down to meet us, and I'm very glad you did. What you need now is a good supper, and when you get back from seeing your dad and mom, you'll have one.''

''Get in the car, Jim,'' Andy ordered, opening the door for me. ''I'm sure you want to see Mom and Dad before you do anything else. It's been a long time since you saw them.''

As we drove through the old neighborhood where I had lived as a boy, I began to think that my life away from home had been only a dream and life here was real.

''I want to caution you,'' Andy warned as we slowed at the house where I had grown up. ''Dad's in a lot of pain much of the time and he takes some pills that sometimes give him a really bad temper. Mom's changed a lot, too. She's aged and has suffered a couple of strokes.''

My heart beat faster as I entered the familiar entrance hall. It seemed smaller and more shabby than I had remembered. Everything in the house still looked familiar. For a moment, I felt as if I had never left.

But the bent old lady who answered the bell didn't look like I remembered my mom. Her hair was white and there were deep wrinkles in her face. One of her cheeks seemed frozenlike. ''Hi, Jim,'' she said as if I were still living at home and had just come back from the store. ''Come in and say hello to your dad.''

Dad was lying in one of the beds in my parents' room. The furniture in the room hadn't changed much, but I recalled that there had been a double bed where the twin beds now stood. Dad's eyes were closed and he was breathing heavy.

It wasn't easy to recognize him. His face looked like it was made out of thin, grey cardboard. His cheeks were sunk in, making his nose look bigger than it had ever been. I recalled how his thick neck and hefty arms had been. He used to threaten to beat me up when I got into trouble at school. I was afraid of him in those days.

I looked at him now. His neck had shrunk and his arms were skinny, ringed with blue veins. I thought what a pushover he'd be if he tried to fight me now. Then something inside of me made me want to cry.

Why had I forgotten the good things my dad had done for me when I was a boy, I wondered. Suddenly, all the reasons I had hated him for seemed to wash down a drain. I felt my arms reaching toward the ghost of a man in the bed. I now wanted to hug him and ask him to hug me. I wanted to tell him, ''Forgive me, Dad. I really love you. Please love me, too.''

My dad's eyes opened slowly and stared into

space. Andy bent over him and said softly, "Dad, Jim has come back to see you." Andy pointed to me standing by the bed. Slowly, Dad turned to look at me. It took a few moments for his eyes to focus. He didn't say anything for a while. I thought that he wasn't able to see me.

When he finally spoke, Dad's voice was harsh though weak. He turned back to Andy. "That no-good son of mine—tell him to get out!" His eyes closed, his head fell back on the pillow, and his heavy breathing continued.

Andy looked at me concerned. He seemed puzzled that I was smiling. How easy it would be to lick him now, I thought.

The meal Andy's wife served that evening was the best I've eaten in my whole life. But I couldn't eat as much as I had expected to. Peggy was disappointed and kept urging me to eat more, telling me I didn't need to be on a diet. I shook my head. I kept looking at my brother, George, across the table. He was there with his wife, a small blond who kept talking to Andy's wife. When Andy had introduced me to her, she moved away from me as if I were a wino asking her for a handout. It was easy to see that George and his wife wanted nothing to do with me.

As I looked around, I thought what a beautiful house Andy had, and how lucky he was to have such a good-looking wife. When I compared myself to him, I felt life had been very unfair to me. Although Andy and his wife, Peggy, tried to make me feel welcome, I didn't feel comfortable in my brother's house. I didn't feel like I belonged in this house or this town. When I thought of what Dad had said to me, I pictured myself choking the rest of his life out of him. As far as I was concerned, Mom was a stranger. I didn't feel any love for her. I wanted to go back to the park where Andy had found me.

After dinner I just sat and said nothing while the others talked about politics, taxes, new books, and a lot of stuff that just didn't interest me. Later, Peggy took me to a guest room which was big, clean, and had a soft rug and expensive-looking furniture. She gave me a pair of pajamas and some towels and showed me where the bathroom was. I noticed that someone had placed a razor and shaving cream near the sink. Seeing them made me look into the mirror at my stubbled face.

When we returned to the guest room, Peggy picked up my blue canvas bag and carried it over to the bed. I saw her look of surprise at how heavy it was. Then she asked me if there was anything else I needed. I shook my head. She wished me a good night and left. I hoped she hadn't guessed what made my bag so heavy.

After she left, I sat on one of the padded chairs in the room for a long time, thinking of how my brothers used to make fun of me when I couldn't make my words come out right. I thought of the teachers who kept me after school for doing things the other kids got away with. I remembered girls I had tried to date turning me down, and how I wished I were dead when they turned away from me. I remembered my mother asking me to be more like Andy and George.

I kept on thinking. The guys I had worked for who fired me would agree with my dad, my brothers, my teachers, and everybody else who knew me—that I was no good. They were wrong! Unfair! I remembered the guys at the railway stations taking away my money and beating me up. They were unfair too! The whole damn world was unfair!

Suddenly I knew I had to get out of my brother's house. I wondered how I could sneak out without anyone hearing me. I grabbed my blue canvas bag and one of the big bathtowels in the bathroom and crept downstairs. Everything was quiet. I went out through the front door, hardly making a sound.

I walked fast till I came to a park at the other end of town. Tired, I stretched out on a bench, draping myself in the towel. My blue canvas bag served as a pillow. It was hard, but comforting. If anyone tried to yank it out from under me, I'd know it. Early in the morning, a policeman woke me up and told me to scram. ''The park benches weren't meant to be used as beds,'' he said sternly. He pointed to the street and told me to get going.

I had enough money for coffee and donuts at a restaurant near the park. It was filled with people going to work. A family with two kids about the age of Andy's kids were having breakfast. They looked tired, as if they had been traveling all night. The hostess who took me to a table somewhere in the back told me that a waitress would be with me soon. I waited for a long time, smelling the coffee. Other people who had come later than I were served coffee as soon as they were seated. The waitress passed right by me, carrying plates with eggs, bacon, and home fries to other tables. Suddenly, I felt something inside of me burst.

My hand dived into my blue canvas bag and grabbed the assault gun, and I let my anger flow through it. As my anger exploded again and again, I felt it ebbing out of me for the first time in my life. I looked around at the people in the restaurant. They weren't strangers—these shapes in the sights of my gun! I knew them all! Everyone I killed was guilty! I knew that hiding within them were my father, my mother, my brothers, my teachers, the girls who wouldn't date me, the guys who beat me up, the bosses who fired me, the cop who chased me out of the park, and the goddamned waitress who wouldn't serve me coffee.

I would have liked to shoot up the whole unfair world. But I couldn't. I had to save the last round for myself.

## FROM A NEWSPAPER EDITORIAL:

It happened again—crazed mass murder! A man went berserk leaving us angry, stunned and confused. Who could have foretold that this monstrous tragedy would happen here in our town? As we mourn the death of the victims, we must ask what could possess a man, coming from a good family, whose brothers are prominent local citizens, to indiscriminately kill eleven innocent people who were total strangers to him.

## COMMENT:

*It is beyond the comprehension of most people that anyone—except a person who is insane—would want to gun down total strangers. The motive for this kind of killing becomes even more baffling when it is committed by a person who has no previous history of violence.*

*Among mass murderers there have been college*

students, people holding good jobs, those from respectable families, as well as those at the bottom socioeconomic levels who were mentally ill or under the influence of drugs or alcohol.

Mass murder would, indeed, be inexplicable if the perpetrator really believed that the people he killed were strangers who had done him no harm. The facts are, however, that in his mind he was acquainted with every one of his victims. In his distorted imagination, his victims were symbols representing people who, throughout his life, had wounded his pride more than he could finally tolerate. His crime is "senseless" to us, but not to him. In the mass murderer's mind, he is at last getting revenge for all the hurts he feels he has suffered throughout his lifetime.

Mass murderers are reacting to a delusional fear, if they are psychotic, or to an overwhelming pent-up rage that has reached an explosive level, if they are not. Psychotic mass killers are in the minority. They believe that their victims are actually enemies against whom they must protect themselves. They suffer from a paranoid delusional disorder. Persons on hallucinogens may also acquire delusions of this type. These are not puzzling cases. Harder to understand is mass murder committed by a person who has exhibited no previous signs of mental illness, but then has a brief reactive psychosis.

In such cases, the person who commits this kind of crime usually suffers from one of the personality disorders within the schizoid, schizotypal, or an associated category. Such persons have no desire for close relationships, lack impulse control, have unstable work histories and, in general, have difficulty

*in getting along. In such a person, inner anger may
build up bit by bit over time, creating symbols upon
which to take revenge for a lifetime of frustration.
Jim was one of these.*

*Jayson decided that he wouldn't share his terrible secret with anyone. His life was warped by the tragedy he refused to reveal. Still, he found something he could be grateful for. It is unlikely that even his psychiatrist could have foretold what that was. It didn't make sense that Jayson wouldn't be grateful for the help offered him. But who ever claimed that a drifter always did things that made sense to other people?*

# JAYSON:
# A "Drifter"

My body chose to stretch itself out across the sidewalk of downtown Elm Street. Had it, instead, preferred to lie along the curb, people wouldn't have had to walk over or around it. In that case, the police might not have been called and I would have rested in peace until I sobered up and disappeared.

The sight of two unsmiling cops had the effect of a pail of water poured over my head.

"What's your name?" they asked me.

"Jayson Sarka."

Satisfied, they escorted me to their police car without asking further questions. Had I confessed theft or robbery, they might have been obliged to lock me up. I knew that they didn't relish having a dirty, unkempt vagrant smelling of cheap wine, occupying a cell in their clean jail. It had been built to house more worthy persons than myself. From past experience I expected to be unloaded at the end of town and sternly advised never to show up again. But this isn't what happened.

As we were driving, the police must have overheard me talking to myself—a form of free entertainment common among street people. To make conversation, I was telling myself that I would be better off dead. I had used poor judgment. What I said was overheard. The two cops in front looked at each other, nodded, and spun the steering wheel around. The car made a sharp U-turn and headed in the opposite direction. I was taken to the psycho ward of the town's regional medical center.

I was admitted. After I had taken a supervised hot shower, I was issued patients' clothing. Except for rare occasions when lodged in shelters for the homeless, I hadn't been this clean for at least ten or more years. I was escorted to a large room in the hospital's locked psychiatric ward and assigned a bed between two sleeping psychos. The next day, I got a physical examination with thumping, prodding, and jabbing that would have earned a bloody nose had one street guy done it to another. I felt like a fish out of water in this place.

From then on, nurses and psychiatric aides kept me busy, ordering me to attend this or that activity. I didn't like being told what to do. I was glad that some of the patients seemed to live in their own crazy worlds. I felt at home with them. They reminded me of some of my fellow street people.

I wasn't in the hospital long before an aide informed me that I had an appointment with the social worker. He walked me to a small office at the rear of the ward. The social worker was a tall, thin woman who greeted me with a brief smile and a nod. After I was seated she told me that she wanted to get some background information on me so that the doctor would know how to help me.

"He can help me most by letting me out of here. There's nothing wrong with me," I told her.

"If you cooperate, you won't be here long," she promised. I got the message. If I didn't cooperate I might be in the crazy-house forever.

The social worker opened one of the folders on her desk. "Your name is Jayson Philip Sarka?" I nodded. For some reason, my name seemed to surprise her. "Isn't 'Jayson' spelled with a 'y' unusual?" she asked, looking at me.

"People call me 'Jay,' " I said. It wasn't the first time the spelling of my name had raised an eyebrow.

"You were born in Brookfield, Pennsylvania and you're thirty-two years old?" The social worker glanced at me again. I didn't answer.

"The police report states that you threatened to commit suicide." I felt my mouth opening in surprise. I wanted to tell her that this was an exaggeration, but she continued talking.

"The law requires the police to send us all persons who threaten to take their own lives, and we are responsible for evaluating them," she explained.

I was afraid of what was coming. I didn't feel like telling her about what had happened to me in my life. I didn't even want to think about the past. But I expected her to persist until she had wrung some facts out of me. I knew that if I cooperated, my stay would be shorter, so I decided to talk. Strangely, once I had started, I found that I really didn't mind talking about myself.

"Do you have an address?"

"The sidewalk of Elm Street," I said. "The police disturbed me in my home and brought me here."

"You have no permanent address?"

"The streets, park benches, and railway yards of the United States," I said, "and once in a while the missions, shelters, and flop houses across our great country."

"Tell me something about your family," the social worker said, ignoring my sarcasm. "How many brothers and sisters do you have?"

"No brothers. I had a sister who died when she was three. I was seven years old at the time."

"Let's talk about your parents. Are you in contact with them?"

"My mother has been dead for many years. I don't know where my father is," I told her. But I knew where he was.

"How would you describe your mother?"

"Mom was a widow when she married Dad." As I said this, a long-forgotten scene flashed through my mind. "After my sister died, Mom had crying spells. Then, sometimes, she'd hug me and say, 'You're the only one I have left out of three.' Mom told me that in her first marriage she had also lost a child. I remember that I had been curious about having had a half-sister or brother I had never known. I asked her for more information, but she turned away and wouldn't talk about it. I stopped asking her, but kept wondering about the half-sister or brother I may have had." The social worker wrote down what I had said.

"Did your mother work outside of your home when you were a child?"

"We needed more money than Dad earned,

but Mom couldn't work. Sometimes, she had to see a doctor because she'd get depressed. But she must have been smart in school. She once told me that she'd won a scholarship to go to college, but turned it down to get married. She and I always got along okay."

"And your father? What kind of work did he do?"

"My dad was a construction worker, often without a job." I hoped that she wouldn't ask me too many questions about him.

"What kind of person was he?"

"He had a quick temper. I didn't like him, and he didn't like me."

"Why was that?" I had anticipated that the social worker would bug me.

"When I was a boy we kept chickens and grew vegetables in the field behind our house. Dad gave me the job of cleaning the henhouse, weeding and fertilizing, and used to yell at me for not doing things his way or fast enough. I couldn't stand him telling me what to do even in those days. Maybe that's why I never could keep a job. I didn't like a boss to tell me what to do."

"And at school, how did you get along with your teachers and the other students?"

"I didn't like the teachers because they also kept telling me what to do. In high school I used to smoke a few joints with some of the guys, but other than that, I didn't have much to do with them.''

''How well did you do in your school work?'' The social worker's pen kept moving on the paper.

''I mostly got A's and B's even though I disliked school and didn't do much studying. Once, when I was tested, they told me that I had a high IQ.''

''With such ability, what happened that caused you to become a drifter?''

I didn't resent her asking me this, but I didn't want to talk about it. Her question brought to mind memories of events that I had kept pushing out of it almost from the time they happened. A picture of the girl who had jilted me swam before my eyes. Then, unable to stop it, I found myself reliving that day when I came home from the library and saw a policeman standing guard at the front door of our house.

''You can't go in right now,'' he told me. ''Detectives are investigating a death.''

Soon I knew the horrible truth. My father, in a frenzy of rage, had killed my mother. I was surprised at how cool I was as I thought about it after all these years. I had no wish to explain that I could handle my restlessness only by moving from place to place, never settling down. I had no intention of sharing my thoughts with the social worker. Some things that had happened in my life are my own to keep.

"Alcohol did it," I replied, shrugging. "I got drunk, stayed drunk, smoked dope and used coke when I could get it."

"And how did you exist—eat, sleep?"

"The way of my breed," I told her, smiling. "Worked at odd jobs when I could; slept where I could; bought food when I had money, and stole it when I didn't, or just went hungry. Here and there I earned handouts and a bed at rescue missions by praying and singing hymns, and stuff like that."

There were more questions. She got it out of me that, sometimes, I get pretty much depressed. She said the doctor might be able to help me with that.

"The medical exam you got after admission showed that you have chronic bronchitis and moderate malnutrition. We don't know what else until the lab reports come back. Still, you are probably lucky. You seem to be in better physical shape than would have been expected with your life-style. A doctor will go over the results of your physical with you later on." I began to jiggle my left leg to relieve my growing restlessness.

"At three, Wednesday, the day after tomorrow, you have an appointment to see Dr. Jordan, our psychiatrist. An aide will remind you." I didn't look forward to a meeting with a psychiatrist, but I knew that I couldn't avoid it.

When I rose to leave, the social worker gave me the same brief smile I'd seen on her face when I entered her office. Again, it looked false to me. But maybe that's just the way social workers smile, I thought.

The staff kept me busy with group therapy, occupational therapy, and recreational therapy, but they couldn't force my mind to be there. I planned to save my mind for my encounter with the psychiatrist. He was the person who would determine when I could leave this place. An aide left me off at his office. A man in a white doctor's coat got up from his chair.

"I'm Dr. Jordan," he introduced himself, and we shook hands. He was a man of about my build. His trim beard was quite unlike my straggly one. He was about fifty I guessed.

"So you are Jayson Philip Sarka," the psychiatrist said, staring at me. I waited for him to say something. He continued to size me up. Finally, he turned his eyes to a folder on his desk.

I felt my face getting red. I hadn't expected

an embarrassing inspection. I'm a new kind of a beast in his zoo, I decided. I must fascinate him.

The psychiatrist turned to me. "I've read your case history. It is very interesting."

He gave the "interesting" a special emphasis. I tried not to show my resentment. I wondered what would happen if I got up and walked out of his office. I'd be locked up in the psycho ward for a long time, I was sure. This guy was important. I had to get along with him, I figured.

"People who survive on the streets don't come here often I guess," I said to break the ice.

"Oh, we have them now and then," Dr. Jordan replied. His head was now stuck into my folder. "What did your sister die of?" he asked when his head came up.

"Probably a cold," I replied, thinking that he might be trying to test my intelligence. I resented it.

"And your mother—what was her life like?"

"Happy. She was always happy," I told him.

For a moment, I thought he would get up and slam me. I warned myself to be careful. The guy is nuts! Judging by his behavior, crazies on the street and psychiatrists in their offices were the same kind of people occupying different places. Worse than nuts, he was, no doubt, a bleeding heart. I hadn't met many of those on the street.

"What can I do for you?" he asked, seeming eager to help me. I had judged him right.

"Frankly, Doctor, I want to get out of this hospital and go back to where I came from."

"The streets?" He looked distressed.

"Yes," I said, loud enough to let him know I meant it. "I don't belong here. I can't stand having people tell me what to do. I may look like a strange animal to you," I felt the muscles of my throat tightening, "but to me, all of you who work at the hospital are the strange ones." I took a deep breath.

"Help me get out of here, Doctor!" I wasn't begging, but it probably sounded as if I were. "I know my rights," I added. "There's nothing wrong with me. You can't keep me here against my will!"

"But I am here to help you." The psychiatrist seemed to be the one who was pleading now. It was ridiculous.

"You are depressed and your mother suffered from depression. You didn't tell the truth when you said that she had been happy. From your records I see that you are intelligent and I want to tell you that there are funds available for rehabilitation. I plan to recommend that you be sent to college. You're not too old for that.''

I looked at him carefully. The whole interview was not what I had expected. Something about him seemed vaguely familiar. It must be that his telling me what to do reminded me of my father. I began to resent him.

''I don't want to go to college!'' I was almost shouting now. ''You have no right to tell me what to do! Get out of my life! You may be my psychiatrist, but I'm not a little kid that has to be told what to do!''

''I'm not just your psychiatrist, Jayson. My name is Jayson Philip Jordan. I am pretty sure that I am also your half brother. The grey eyes of the man across the desk looked into mine of the same color.

''Repeat that!'' I demanded, not understanding what he meant.

The psychiatrist leaned back in his chair. For the first time I became aware of how stressed he looked.

''Your name made me curious, and when I read your file, it confirmed what I had suspected. My own father was killed in an automobile accident a few months before I was born. I am certain that your mother was also my birth mother. She gave me up for adoption. She had been hospitalized for postpartum psychosis and a history of depression. Dad's death and having a new baby was more than she could handle at that time.''

He had a need to talk. ''A family named Jordan adopted me. They kept the name mother had given me, Jayson Philip. My new parents gave me love and provided for my education all the way through medical school. They let me know early in life that I had been adopted. As a child, sometimes I lived with my birth mother in fantasy. Later I kept alive a love for her.''

Was I dreaming? Was this psychiatrist making this all up? I asked myself what reason he would have to do so. I tried to pull myself together. ''If you were adopted as a baby, how could you be so sure that we're related?'' I asked him.

''After I got through medical school I made up my mind to locate my birth mother. It took a bit of doing, but I found that she had married a man with the last name of Sarka who lived in Brookfield, Pennsylvania, near Pittsburgh. The rest was easy. I wrote her and then met her once. I visited her while you were in school and your father was at work.''

''Our birth mother was a sweet woman, but somehow I thought, sad,'' he continued. She told me that it was her love for me that made her give me up so that I could have the chance to make the most of myself. I could accept that.'' The psychiatrist paused. He seemed to be with my mother, far away.

I could hardly believe that he was reliving such an emotional experience with my own mother. I found myself having both anger and a warm feeling toward him.

''She was very proud when I told her that I had become a doctor,'' he continued. ''She said my visit had made her happy. She told me that she had never forgotten me and had always loved me. In order never to forget me, she gave you the same given names as mine.'' The psychiatrist was staring at the rug, seeming to be deep in thought.

I tried to imagine what Mom would think of me if she were alive. Without a doubt, that I was a failure, but that at least one of her sons was a success. I looked at the man sitting across from me and felt jealous. So, Mom had given me his name, I thought, feeling bitter.

''I see from your interview with the social worker,'' my half brother said turning to me, ''our mother died a number of years ago. What caused her death?''

I held my breath. The chance to get even with him had fallen into my lap. I had him now! The terrible truth would haunt him all of his life! I glanced at his familiar-looking eyes.

''Our doctor said she died of natural causes.''

"Good! I was afraid it might have been otherwise." I watched his face relax. "Now, as for you," he continued, "after your discharge from the hospital we're going to send you for rehabilitation to an alcoholic treatment center. You can be sure that we'll keep tabs on your taking the medication that has been prescribed for your depression. Next, you'll go for vocational evaluation to find out what kind of occupational training would be appropriate for you."

Brotherly love was a new experience for me. I began to sweat.

"Tomorrow, I'll arrange for you to take an afternoon's leave of absence from the hospital. I want Debbie, my wife, to meet her long lost half brother-in-law—can one call it that? Let's see when I can arrange this." My half brother consulted the heavily pencilled calendar on his desk.

"I am working late tonight and tomorrow so it can't be then. Friday evening I'm slated to give a lecture on aging to a senior citizens' group. Saturday and Sunday I'm on call, and I know I'll be busy. Let's make it Monday night. No, I promised the staff at the nursing home I'd be there to answer questions on Alzheimer's disease. And Tuesday? Isn't it in-service training day?" He consulted his calendar again and nodded.

I didn't tell him not to waste his time. Soon

I would be back on the streets—free—taking the medication of my choice, from a bottle, with the street people like me.

My half brother furrowed his brow as he continued leafing through his calendar.

I heard him sigh and told myself, pitying him, "There but for the grace of God sit I." I wasn't sure there was a God, but in case there was, I raised my eyes gratefully toward the ceiling.

## COMMENT:

*Who are the "street people"? In some ways Jayson was typical of some of them—those from dysfunctional families who experienced neglect, trauma, or rejection from either one or both parents or a significant other person. Most of them are as disillusioned and cynical about society as Jayson was. They may suffer from one or a combination of personality disorders causing them to reject society and live only on its fringes.*

*Over a period of time almost all vagrants are apt to fall prey to one or, usually, several chronic illnesses. These result from malnutrition, unsanitary living conditions, substance abuse, and exposure to harsh weather. Likewise, many so-called "drifters," "transients," or "street people" suffer from mental illnesses ranging from schizophrenia to organic brain pathology. Alcoholism and drug abuse are rampant among this entire population.*

A recent census has revealed a moderate number of these people were basically normal—at least when they began living on the streets. Unfortunate circumstances may have forced them there, such as loss of assets, unemployment, divorce, or a loss of a support system.

There are skilled people among the homeless who could find employment if they were able to organize their lives. An increasing number of older men and women who have lost a spouse and no longer have sufficient coping ability have joined the ranks of the homeless. It is sad that there are people living on the street who are entitled to various benefits but are unaware of them or unable to contact an appropriate agency to receive help.

Dr. Jordan can hardly be blamed for losing his objectivity when he found that he had a half brother among the patients on the psychiatric ward. We can be certain that not many street people are offered the opportunities that were extended to the younger Jayson. Dr. Jordan apparently did not anticipate that the "drifter" with whom he shared a biological mother would turn down his offer for rehabilitation, education, and a family relationship. Nor would the psychiatrist have expected that his half brother would watch him thumb through the calendar on his desk and think, gratefully, "There but for the grace of God sit I."

*Douglas longed for the peace that Jerry, his psychologist, said would follow resignation. He wondered how he could resign himself to having AIDS when his friends were dying from it. Instead of resignation, Douglas felt only mounting panic. Peace, he was sure, was out of his reach.*

# DOUGLAS:
# Positive for HIV

For months I hadn't felt well. Now I sat in the doctor's office trying not to think. My eyes were glued on the door. The door opened and the doctor entered. When he saw me he seemed to hesitate and directed his eyes at the floor. Then I knew I had AIDS. "You tested positive for HIV—I'm sorry." His eyes met mine now.

My worst fears were confirmed. I felt only bones, muscles, and ligaments in my body. There was no brain to give it understanding.

"Things aren't quite as hopeless as they used to be." I heard the doctor's words. He was talking to someone else who—it dawned on me slowly—was also me.

"A great deal of good research is going on these days to find new drugs to fight Acquired

Immune Deficiency Syndrome. For a starter, I'll write you a prescription for Retrovir. You've probably heard it referred to as AZT. It's most effective if taken early in the course of the disease. We've learned that it's important that you keep fighting your illness with your mind. We have come a long way in delaying the secondary infections, but more and more we find that the patient's mental state is crucial."

"Thanks, Doctor." I was surprised to hear myself speaking.

The doctor was businesslike now. "Before you leave today, I have a rather detailed questionnaire I'd like you to fill out. I am sorry that I have to ask you to do this. It is essential that you are as frank and accurate as possible when you answer the questions."

I understood what he was saying, yet, somehow, it seemed meaningless.

"Stop at the desk and make an appointment to see me in about two weeks," the doctor continued. "In the meantime, I'm going to make some referrals for you with people who will tell you what you must do for your own safety and the safety of others." He handed me a pamphlet. "Read this carefully, Doug. Keep a list of any questions you have." He squeezed my shoulder, got up, and left.

I filled out the questionnaire in the waiting

room. About an hour later I was on the street again. It seemed to me that everything was far away—buildings, cars, people. Even the houses I passed on my way to the patients' parking lot didn't really seem to be there. A cloud of "me-ness" enveloped and numbed me. It blurred my thinking and feeling.

I drove my 1987 Honda home and parked on the street in front of my small apartment. Joseph and I had lived there until he left me a couple of months ago. I crawled into bed not totally aware of what I was doing.

The moment I closed my eyes, questions penetrated my protecting cloud of "me-ness." Do I really have AIDS after all the precautions I have taken? Couldn't there have been a mistake? Am I really going to die?

A part of my mind answered, "The lab technicians have you mixed up with someone else!" My mind accepted this as reasonable. I decided I would call the doctor early tomorrow and ask him to check my lab records again. Then hopelessness came from somewhere—a blanket smothering a tiny flame. What will it feel like to die? Another thought broke into the hopelessness. Maybe a cure will be discovered before I die! I drifted off to sleep.

When I woke up, I glanced at the clock on the dresser and was surprised to see that it was 9:00 P.M. I had slept for four hours. It felt good to stretch. "How long will I be able to stretch?" I asked myself, suddenly remembering, "I won't allow myself to think like that!" I said aloud, clenching my teeth. I took a deep breath and reached down to masturbate. Escape, what beautiful escape that would be. But, damn it, I couldn't.

Tears of frustration started to fill my eyes, but I pushed them back. I became aware that my brain seemed to be making a cautious effort to rejoin the rest of me. My brain reminded me that I was still one of the best waiters at the restaurant even though, often, I wasn't feeling completely well. And—I almost smiled—I was still making more tips than anyone else there.

The doctor had given me names of people and organizations that offered emotional support to persons with AIDS. I had no wish to confide in them. I asked myself, "Whom shall I tell that I have AIDS? Not my parents, not my sister, not the guys at work. Nobody!" I answered aloud, my eyes starting to mist again. "Nobody—except the bastard who had infected me!" I started breathing hard. I fought an overpowering urge to find whoever he was and kill him! "What good would it do?" I asked aloud. "Is it because I'm gay?" A fraction of a second later I was ashamed that I had had that stupid thought. Plenty of straights were getting AIDS, too.

It was close to midnight, but I couldn't fall asleep. In my mind I kept picturing my parents sitting in their living room, but I was unable to read their expressions. I remembered that they had often disapproved of some of the things I used to do. "Please be loving and kind," I begged them as I imagined them listening. "Remember, I'm your only son!" As the picture of my parents faded, I saw some of my life played backwards in my mind, like a videotape in a VCR rewinding on the television screen. I tried to turn it off, but couldn't.

With so much on my mind, it was hard to remember some of the orders people at the restaurant gave me when I served them. But it wasn't until I got home each night that my behavior seemed to go entirely out of whack. Like the night I was in bed and felt my arm fling itself above my head as if it had been yanked by a robot. It came down full force and slammed into my pillow. "That won't get you anywhere!" I told myself, feeling pain in my arm from the jolt.

On another night, while in bed and staring into the darkness, an eerie sense of power came over me. I was aware that I could kill people with just the tiniest portion of a single drop of my blood. I thought that if I did so just before I died, it wouldn't matter if I got caught. Usually, more practical considerations crossed my mind. How would I live? How would I die?

I thought of my friend, Mark, who hadn't been able to work for the past few months. I recalled how I had pitied him when I first heard that he had contracted AIDS. How certain I had been then that it couldn't happen to me. Recently, I heard that Mark was recovering from some real serious kind of pneumonia that people with AIDS can get. I knew that it was usually fatal. "But Mark is *recovering*," I told myself, finding a ray of hope in that.

The months went by. I was grateful that I could continue on my job. It isn't easy to be a waiter when one isn't feeling great, but it was comforting to be among people I knew and trusted. In time, I found myself more content. Between the various appointments my doctor kept setting up for me, I could even forget, at times, that I had AIDS. But, always, when I seemed close to regaining some happiness, depression would return. So far my depression hadn't been serious enough to let me down for too long. "Don't think of tomorrow!" I told myself. "Live day by day."

With time, it was no longer important not to tell anyone that I had AIDS. The ice had been broken when I attended a "Disclosure Meeting" in my neighborhood. A social worker had talked to a small group of us about "precautions" and "attitudes." She gave us a list of counselors who specialized in providing ongoing guidance to people with AIDS. On the list was a psychologist, a Dr. Lee, who, I was glad to note, was employed by the union to which I belong. I decided to call him for an appointment.

When I arrived at Dr. Lee's office, I found myself in a room that was almost bare. The furniture consisted of two chairs, a desk, and a couple of filing cabinets. Instead of certificates, there was only a lonesome picture of a cornfield hanging on the wall. It showed three trees growing inappropriately in the middle of the field. The picture hung at an angle behind the tall, thin man who rose from his desk as I entered. He shook my hand and told me he was "Jerry."

Jerry must have noticed me looking around the room when I first entered. "We're bare bones here," he remarked, smiling and looking around. "People who have AIDS, like you and I, aren't impressed by luxury. I guess you could say we're down to basics."

"Like you and *I*" My eyes searched for his pain or self-pity. There was none.

"I'll start by giving you a little orientation," Jerry said after I sat down. "I'm a psychologist and I will work closely with your physician. He has probably told you that your state of mind will affect the strength of your resistance to the virus."

I nodded. "But I can't help feeling depressed," I told him. "And sometimes I get crazy thoughts!"

"You wouldn't be human if you didn't," Jerry replied. "Worse than not being human," he added, "you would be using denial. And that's not always good."

He changed the subject. "Let me tell you something about our union. You are fortunate to belong to it, although there are now other groups and organizations that do similar things for AIDS patients. We have close to 12,000 members. Presently, forty members have AIDS. They can no longer work and are receiving monthly supplements. These supplements mean the difference between maintaining a relatively normal life-style and homelessness. It's not only the money, but the services and support we provide that help."

As Jerry paused, I looked at him. I wondered whether he had contracted AIDS from a blood transfusion. Curiously, it didn't matter. Another AIDS victim is a brother or sister no matter how the infection occurred. It was ironic that no effort to give humans a common identity has ever been as successful as the HIV virus.

As our sessions continued, I realized that, so far, I had been more or less able to maintain my level of health. I began to hope that I was one of the lucky ones who wouldn't succumb quickly to the disease. I wondered if my sessions with Jerry were helping me to sustain my health. I would now be able to share my fears and hopes without holding anything back. I was amazed at his ability to sense my moods and relate to each of them without even asking me to describe how I felt.

Jerry told me one day when we were discussing the seemingly unreasonable anger that had been building up within me for several weeks, "I also used to blame the world for having tested positive to HIV. Anger is one of the stages most of us pass through. It follows initial disbelief. Anger usually gives way to depression and, with time, it is often replaced by resignation. With resignation comes the special kind of peace that is reserved for those who have suffered deeply."

I couldn't remember going through all of the stages that Jerry described. "I had all of those feelings scrambled up together from the beginning," I told him after thinking about it. "I'll never reach a stage of resignation! How can anyone be resigned to having AIDS?"

"It's healthy not to feel resigned prematurely," Jerry replied. "Resignation isn't giving up. There are some people who had inner peace long before they ever got sick. But for most of us, achieving resignation is our reward for having fought. Peace, then, is the reward one gets from resignation."

"Peace?" I thought with a longing that sprang from somewhere deep within me.

"Peace?" I felt that it was totally out of my reach.

I don't exactly recall when I began to notice that Jerry wasn't looking very well. I could see that he had lost weight and was coughing a lot. I wasn't surprised when I was told that he had been hospitalized. It shook me, however, to hear, two weeks later, that he had died. I felt that I had lost the best friend I had ever had.

I went to the library and looked up the symptoms of "opportunistic infections," which is something AIDS patients get, and looked up the complications in the medical books. I scoured newspapers and magazines for reports of breakthroughs in the treatment of AIDS. I was alone most of the time now. Friends I had made at the meetings I used to attend were drifting away. Joe was in a hospice with pneumocistic pneumonia. Theresa was hospitalized with Kaposi's sarcoma. Mark and Jerry had recently died. I asked myself, "How can I be resigned when my friends are dying of the disease I also have." Instead of resignation, I felt only mounting panic.

During the months that slowly passed, the doctor had to prescribe dietary supplements because the medications I was taking had made me anemic. I developed a fungal infection and was also on medication for the diarrhea which was sapping my strength. I found now that working had become too much of an effort. I was able to live on Medicare and the pension I received from the union. Some days I found it difficult to even get out of bed in the morning and was tired much of the day.

"Fight!" everyone urged me. "Cheer on your immune system and give your T cells and their helper cells encouragement!" But I couldn't do it. Perhaps, I thought, I could have fought it if Jerry were alive to help me.

It seemed to me now that one look at me was enough for anyone in the neighborhood to see that I had AIDS. People in the apartment building where I lived kept their distance and lowered their eyes when they passed me. Yesterday, while I was buying a few things at the supermarket, a mother pulled her child away from where I was standing. I felt that people were avoiding me everywhere—even people who couldn't have known that I had AIDS.

Every day I examined myself carefully. I kept watching several blue spots on my legs. I planned to try to move up my appointment with the doctor because I thought maybe I had found the first signs of sarcoma on my body. Still, I couldn't imagine myself resigned to dying. Perhaps I hadn't yet emerged from the angry state Jerry and I had talked about. And yet, "anger" didn't fit the way I felt. I thought that the English language was deficient in vocabulary for people who have AIDS.

There should be a word that stands for anger, fear, and depression all rolled into one. There needs to be a word to describe the attempt to encourage an immune system that isn't working. Perhaps more than any other, we need a word that means trying to act cheerful while wishing to get it over with—fighting for life while longing for death.

As I began to feel worse, I didn't want to remain angry. Impatiently now, I waited for the peace Jerry had said some people find near the end of the road. But I remembered that peace had to be earned. It came to those who fought hard enough to deserve the peace I longed for.

Suddenly, I remembered that I had an appointment to see the doctor in less than an hour. He wanted to check me over and give me a prescription for a different kind of antibiotic. I quickly dressed, got into my car, and headed out. I froze at the steering wheel when, suddenly, out of the corner of my eye I saw a speeding car coming out of nowhere and heading toward me—like a bolt of lightening!

Newspaper Headline on Page 8

MAN ON WAY TO DOCTOR KILLED BY DRUNKEN DRIVER

According to witnesses, a green pickup sped

through a red light and broadsided another car driven by Douglas Herrick, age 27, killing him instantly. Herrick was on his way to see his doctor. The driver of the pickup was booked for vehicular manslaughter and driving while intoxicated.

## COMMENT:

*The gamut of emotions Doug experienced isn't unique to persons with AIDS, but may occur to anyone faced with a terminal illness. Typical responses to life-threatening illnesses include reactions also seen in bereavement—depression, poor appetite, weight loss, and insomnia. These symptoms are of a psychological origin and are not caused by the illness directly. Identical symptoms may be the product of the illness itself.*

*Symptoms of Post-traumatic Stress Disorder are often present as well. These may include recurring distressing dreams related to the illness, feelings of detachment or estrangement, restricted range of interests, ongoing anger, and depression. As would be expected, some characteristics of adjustment disorders—anxiety, ambivalence, feelings of hopelessness—are frequently found. Unless the grieving behavior gets completely out of hand, these common reactions to terminal illnesses, or to the death of a loved one, are not abnormal psychiatric conditions.*

*Public attention to the AIDS epidemic is constantly growing. In a recent Roper poll of randomly selected American adults, 81% of those questioned believed that AIDS is among the major problems facing the nation, and 80% gave it priority over cancer, heart disease, alcoholism, and diabetes.*

*Current efforts to contain the AIDS epidemic include increased education on how the disease is transmitted, and intensified research for new drugs. The effort to develop a vaccine to immunize uninfected people against AIDS continues. It is more difficult to find ways to immunize people against AIDS than to other viral diseases because the Human Immunodeficiency Virus attacks the immune system itself.*

*Douglas described the emotional turmoil that some endure who suffer from a prolonged terminal illness. He did it from the human point of view of the victims. The hope is strong that some day there may be a better solution for people suffering from AIDS than the one that, at last, brought peace to Douglas.*

*The psychologist seemed to warm up to the subject. "Most people who are disturbed by their gender identity can handle it without resorting to surgical intervention," he said. Mervin, however, had made up his mind to become a complete woman, body as well as soul. But when he became Mary, were there lingering doubts?*

# MERVIN/MARY:
# A Sign of Success

My sister knew that I wanted to have a surgical sex change. I'm her brother, younger by ten months. She supported my decision reluctantly. I had already made out-of-town appointments for the preliminary psychiatric and medical evaluations that are required before one can be accepted for this kind of surgery. For a while, now, my sister had been urging me to make an appointment with a local mental health specialist. She thought it might be sensible to have a therapist on hand for "future eventualities" as she put it. I agreed. I expected a psychologist to try to discourage me from going ahead with my plans—to be a devil's advocate, so to speak. I thought that the experience would give me a chance to test my resolve. I selected a young psychologist just starting a private practice. I wanted new blood—as raw a material as I could get.

At the psychologist's office I filled out the inevitable preliminary information form and waited to be called. After I was seated in his office that still smelled of new paint, I found myself facing a young man who looked—if not exactly uneasy—a bit uncomfortable. His precisely trimmed black moustache, conservative suit, and his just slightly forced professional manner made me think that he was fresh out of doctoral training and internship.

I thought it might be somewhat unsettling for him to have as one of his first clients a person who wanted to undergo a surgical sex change. Certainly, it wasn't the usual type of problem suburban therapists in private practice expect when they are just starting out.

"You graduated from college last year? You are a woman, somehow mistakenly locked into the body of a man?" He was looking at the form I had filled out. "Did you feel this way before you went to college?"

"I was sure that I was meant to be a girl even before I went to high school," I told him. "As far back as I can remember, I felt that it was wrong for me to have a boy's body."

"And you want to have sex-change surgery?" There was a barely noticeable rise in his voice.

"Yes, it's very necessary for me. I'm sure of it."

"You are aware, of course, that you will require extensive mental and medical evaluation before you can be accepted for this type of surgery?"

"I know."

"And it will be very expensive. No insurance covers it."

"When my grandfather died he left each of his grandchildren a considerable sum of money."

"If you're sure that it's what you want, why did you come to consult me?"

I realized that it was a reasonable question. Nevertheless, I wondered if he was trying to get rid of me. "I wanted someone who is professionally trained to discuss with me, objectively, what I am going to do," I told him.

"I see." His eyes narrowed. Cynically, I guessed he was trying to recall the maximum amount of compensation his malpractice insurance would pay.

"If there is one thing a psychologist is not likely to do without overwhelming evidence indicating that it is necessary, is to recommend castration and surgical feminization," he said, grimly.

"Does that mean you will not accept me as a client?"

"No, that's not so. I am willing to talk with you objectively."

"I may be looking for reassurance," I admitted. "If I changed my mind after castration, breast augmentation, and a surgically created vagina, it probably would take some pretty innovative surgery to restore things."

The psychologist's jaw dropped ever so slightly. For a moment he looked preoccupied, as if absorbed in a mind-boggling mechanical puzzle.

"Recently, however," I said, breaking into his train of thought, "I read that there is plastic surgery for building and rebuilding penises. I guess that's for people with problems opposite to mine." Did I see his eyes drift heavenward just the least bit?

He decided to change the subject. "What was your major in college?" I felt he asked that to reduce the tension that had risen between us.

"Psychology," I replied.

The tension was not reduced. "Psychology?" An almost imperceptible frown creased his brow.

"Yes, I'm preparing myself to be a clinical child psychologist. I have always been a caring person, and I would love to work with children.''

''It is a rewarding area of psychology,'' he agreed, and returned to the subject at hand. ''Most people who are disturbed by their gender identity can handle it in various ways without resorting to surgical intervention. You've thought about this of course.''

I sighed audibly. I had heard all this before.

He seemed to warm up to the subject now. ''There are several different kinds of sexual disorders in which cross-dressing is done for sexual arousal. There is no wish for surgical intervention.''

''Dressing in women's clothes doesn't arouse me sexually,'' I replied. ''I want surgery to correct a mistake nature made. I have a woman's interests, a woman's feelings, a woman's mentality, or whatever you want to call it. I'm a male only on the outside. You can't put a cat into the skin of a dog and expect it to bark!'' The psychologist seemed to think this over.

''Do you think that it is possible that your study of psychology has trapped you into thinking that you have transsexualism which could have come from—or was reinforced by—reading about it?'' he asked.

''No, not at all,'' I replied. ''It's more like a

matter of honesty—like not living a lie.'' My eyes searched his. ''Can't you see the woman in me?'' I asked him.

He ignored the question. He didn't have to answer it. I had looked into mirrors often enough to know that my small mouth and delicate chin were typically feminine. My eyes were large and blue. A few years back I had most of my facial hair removed by electrolysis. Unfortunately, I had my father's nose, a bit large and masculine, but not enough to raise suspicion when I'm dressed in women's clothes. Anyhow, I could always take care of that, I thought.

''There are men without feminine features who want to have sex-change surgery.'' He had guessed my thoughts. ''They require extensive hormonal treatment if they go through with it. On the other hand, there are some men who could pass for women who have no problems of sex identity. Undergoing a surgical sex change is a formidable, irreversible decision.''

''So is suicide,'' I said quietly. The psychologist turned to look at me closer.

''I've tried it twice,'' I said. ''After I slashed my wrists last year, I almost bled to death before my sister found me. I was rushed to a hospital and taken to the emergency room.'' I pulled up my right sleeve to show him the scar. The psychologist studied it silently.

''Was your sexual identity problem the only

reason you made a suicide attempt? Perhaps there were also other problems that contributed to your death wish."

I looked directly at him. "Doctor, there was nothing besides the rejections I got from my parents and others when they found out I wanted to become a complete woman. I can tell you, honestly, as I told them, I'd rather be dead than be imprisoned in a man's body permanently." I closed my eyes to hold back my tears.

"I see," the psychologist said slowly, as if he were viewing me in a new light. "It is important for me to know whether you are still thinking seriously about taking your own life. Would you be frank with me about this?" His look of concern was unmistakable. Rapport between us, absent at first, seemed to have established itself.

"I am not presently planning to kill myself," I told him. The psychologist now asked for facts. "At what age did you start thinking of yourself as a girl?"

"When I was about eight or nine years old I always played with my sister and her friends. I used to cuddle her dolls. I never enjoyed playing with toys made for boys."

"Would you say that your sister had a great influence on your life?" the psychologist asked me.

"She wanted a little sister instead of the brother she got. When her friends came over we used to sit around and talk about girl things. I always felt I belonged with the girls," I explained. "I never felt comfortable with boys. My mother didn't mind, but my father wrote me off as permanently disqualified for his companionship. He was a 'man's man' as they say. Dad and my older brother were more like pals than father and son."

"And when did you start wearing girls' clothing?"

"Even as a small child I would dress up in my sister's clothes. My mother thought it was a game my sister and I were playing. Mother used to laugh and say that I'd probably be an actor and go on stage when I grew up. My father didn't bother to look at me."

The clock was pointing to the end of the session. I hadn't told the psychologist that before I made an appointment with him, I had already made arrangements to begin the psychiatric and medical evaluations that are required for acceptance for sex-change surgery. I decided to share this with him in my next session the following week.

I left his office feeling that the psychologist had put his finger on my secret, nagging doubt. Had I brainwashed myself by reading psychiatric descriptions of transsexualism? I shut the thought out of my mind.

SECOND  SESSION:

When I was again seated in the psychologist's office, I told him that before I had come to consult him last week, I had already taken the first steps to have sex-change surgery, and I gave him the name of the clinic and the city where I had my appointments.

"Uhuh." It was the neutral therapist's grunt, not the words of surprise I had expected.

"You seem to be very sure that you have all the characteristics of transsexualism," he said slowly.

"Yes, and I am going to request a statement from you to that effect," I told him thinking that it might help me in the evaluation I was scheduled to have.

"I can't do that. There are some things that don't fit the picture," he said softly.

The rapport we had established flew out the window. "That's not true!" I felt myself tightening. "I looked it up in the psychiatric manual!"

"Is it possible that your reading about it might explain why your symptoms fit the diagnosis of transsexualism almost too well?"

"I don't understand!" I was becoming more and more upset.

"We agreed to discuss your problem objectively," he reminded me.

I looked at him. His arms were folded, his head inclined. "You tell me that before you came to see me you had already made an appointment to be evaluated for the surgery. Consulting me after you went that far doesn't make sense. Doesn't it mean that you have lingering doubts? If this is true, shouldn't you give your decision second thoughts?" He kept his voice low, trying not to upset me.

"Quite the contrary is true," I replied, recalling why I had come to see him. "I wanted to test myself by talking about my plans with a mental health specialist before I had my required psychiatric evaluation. When I told you about my plan, you were generally negative, as I had expected you would be. But this hasn't changed my mind. Now I feel even more sure of myself. It makes me feel better about it."

The psychologist said that he could see my point. He asked me if I had family members or friends I could count on for emotional support in case I was told that I was ineligible for the surgery.

As I thought about this, it became clear to me that I would have only my sister to turn to if that happened. Bitterly, I realized that people who have my problem are really misunderstood and alone. It is no wonder that we become depressed.

The psychologist said that he would be glad

to see me if I wished to come back to him in the future.

As soon as I arrived at my apartment, I telephoned my sister and told her that her suggestion that I consult a mental health specialist had proven to be a good one.

After my psychiatric examination was completed, I was thrilled to learn that surgery had been approved. I was started on hormone therapy and told that I might have to continue it for the rest of my life. My voice began to settle at a higher pitch and there were breast implants as well as a series of spaced operations. Months passed. Then came more operations with ongoing therapy and more observations. Still more months passed. Gruesome, frightening, exhilarating. Nightmares and happy daydreams, thrilling, liberating—a blessed rebirth! I had come to the clinic as "Mervin." After many trips back and forth, I was "Mary." During this time I had taken legal steps to change my name.

How often did I, now Mary, study my face and body in my full-length mirror at home? There was no doubt about it. From head to toe—I was a woman. For some reason I no longer had the desire to become a child psychologist. Instead, I found a job as a bookkeeper, my college minor. After life had settled down to a routine, I took an evening course in art history, just for fun. I also found myself wanting to visit the psychologist I had consulted before my surgery.

I finally called and made an appointment. I used my new name and didn't mention that I had seen him before. I got prettied up and put on one of my most becoming dresses. I could feel my heart beating fast as I walked into his office. Its tempo quickened when he stared at me.

"Mervin, you did it!" He almost bit his lip. "Mary," he quickly corrected himself. "I congratulate you. You look great!"

As we talked a while, I confessed that, occasionally, I had a few secret fears that I hadn't been able to eradicate all the masculine traces of my former self. I admitted that he had shocked me when he had recognized me as "Mervin."

The psychologist smoothed that over as merely a "mental set" on his part. "You look every bit a woman," he assured me.

"I haven't had sex as a woman yet," I told him, aware of the pang of fear as I said it.

"Do you have an urge for sex?"

"It's not that. I don't recall ever having had a strong urge for sex before or after my surgery. But I think that I would feel better about myself if a man would make love to me—not for the sex, but for the reassurance it would give me.''

I looked at him questioningly, wanting him to tell me not to be afraid. He misunderstood and paled.

''I have someone in mind,'' I said quickly. ''He's in my evening art history class. I missed a few classes when I had the flu. He was especially nice in helping me make up what I had missed. I am planning to try to interest this man in going to bed with me. I would like to be able to talk with you about how it goes.'' We agreed that I would call him for an appointment after my date and I did so.

When I entered the psychologist's office, I began to cry before he could even close the door. I could hardly wait to tell him what had happened.

''I invited the guy I told you about from my class to my apartment to see a book I had bought on the classical period of Greek art. He had once told me that the sculpture of this period was his favorite. At first it was very pleasant. We had a few drinks, discussed art, and joked about our fellow students.

''I had purposely put the book on the dresser in my bedroom. After a while I excused myself, went into the bedroom, and quickly got out of my clothes. I slipped into my new silk robe, tied it loosely, and gave myself a spritz of perfume for good luck. I returned to the living room smiling, sat down next to him, and casually put my arm around him. He asked me where the book on Greek art was. Coyly, I led him into the bedroom.

"I almost died with fright as I untied the belt and let my robe fall to my feet. I stood naked in front of him and said, 'While you're here, let's have some fun.' I glanced at him and saw him watching me. His look just didn't strike me right. I made a few suggestive wiggles. He stared at me and seemed interested. I began to be more hopeful. Still, there was something academic about the way he inspected me. With my heart pounding, I started pulling him toward me.

" 'Sorry, I am gay,' he said, backing away and reaching for the book on my dresser."

"After he left, I almost collapsed," I told the psychologist, sobbing. "Never in my life have I been so humiliated!"

"And you are very much upset at what happened?" he asked, surprisingly unsympathetic.

"It was so difficult to get myself to that stage," I said. "And then—well, it was devastating! Heartbreaking!"

"You were lucky! It was the best evidence you could have gotten that your operation was successful. What conclusion would you have reached, in retrospect, if a gay man had shown sexual interest in you?''

## COMMENT:

*The three primary sexual disorders in which cross-dressing occurs are Transvestism, Gender Identity Disorder, and Transsexualism.*

*Males who are Transvestites have sexual urges that are aroused by dressing in women's clothes. Persons with Gender Identity Disorder experience intense discomfort in having the gender of their birth. Cross-dressing is not done for sexual excitement as in Transvestism.*

*Only Transsexuals desire to rid themselves of their primary and secondary sexual characteristics so that they may acquire the characteristics of the other sex. For the diagnosis of transsexualism there must have been a preoccupation with changing one's gender for at least two years. A sex change requires long, drawn-out evaluations and surgery, which may continue for up to six or more years as described in Mary's narrative.*

*In creating a male to female sex change, hormone therapy, followed by a series of major operations on the genitourinary tract, is necessary. Prosthetic breasts may have to be implanted. The erectile tissue of the penis is removed and repositioned in the urethra. The lining of the vagina is constructed out of the skin of the penis. After the testes have been detached, the skin is used to make the labia.*

*A female to male sex change involves a mastectomy and the removal of the uterus and ovaries. A penis, formed by grafting an abdominal skin flap over a catheter, is then attached. According to the* Diagnostic and Statistical Manual of Mental Disorders (Third Edition–Revised). *Washington, D.C.: American Psychiatric Association, 1987.Transsexualism is one per 30,000 for males and one per 100,000 for females.*

*While I was writing this narrative, an article appeared in the local newspaper headlined "Sex Change Spurs Suit." It stated, "A decorated war veteran was fired as an airline pilot after sex-change surgery. The pilot stated, 'This was a gender problem not a problem with my ability to perform work of any kind. I'm a better pilot because I'm no longer troubled by the feeling of being a woman trapped in a man's body.' "*

*Those astounded by the variety of twists and turns taken by human nature may recall that "truth is often stranger than fiction."*

*Melissa has bulimia. Judging by the number of articles on this disorder these days, it seems that gastronomically inclined voyeurs looking for titillation may find it by reading about this subject. Mental health researchers have shown renewed interest in food bingeing. These developments have contributed to lifting bulimia out of its former obscurity. Yet the victims of this enigmatic eating disorder shun publicity. The less people know about their secret gorging followed by self-induced vomiting, the better bulimics like it.*

# MELISSA:
# In and Out

My name is Melissa. I'm 22 years old, work as a teller in a bank, and live by myself in a small apartment. I graduated from junior college and, after I found a job, I moved out of my parents' home. I keep in touch with them by phone and visits.

One afternoon at the bank an old, grumpy customer with a reputation for frugality handed me a check for an unusually large amount of money made out to "Cash." As long as I had been at the bank, he'd made only a few small withdrawals. I stared at his check, lost consciousness, and slumped to the floor, his check in hand. Everyone at the bank insisted that I had fainted in shock. The doctor in the emergency room at the hospital thought otherwise.

I regained consciousness in the ambulance. ''Low blood sugar'' was the doctor's diagnosis after I admitted that I had been dieting on a small glass of orange juice, a few crackers, and one egg a day. He examined me, drew blood, and admitted me to a hospital that had an eating disorder research program.

The next morning a group of doctors making rounds came to see me. They asked me if I ever binged on food. I told them that I did. ''Bulimarexia,'' the woman doctor who seemed to be in charge whispered to the others. ''We'll check for complications,'' I heard her say.

I was transferred to another floor and put into a room with a young woman who greeted me with, ''Welcome to Bulimialand. I'm Olga, and I'm a student at the State U. In the next room there's Mildred and Stephanie. Stephanie is a fellow sufferer at the U.'' I learned later that Mildred lived at home with her parents, and had a history of drug abuse.

''With you, there are four of us in our eating disorder sorority. At this place they use what they call ''cognitive-behavioral therapy'' for problems like ours. It's a mind/muscle/impulse control mix that the doctors say has proven successful in the past.'' Olga crossed her fingers and looked heavenward, blinking her eyes. I immediately liked Olga and envied her tall, slim figure.

That afternoon I had an appointment with the social worker. She was a young, bony, little woman with bright blue eyes and blonde curly hair. I thought that she must be dieting to be so wonderfully slim. She smiled a welcome and explained that she used an informal approach to interviewing. "If you wish, you could start by describing your childhood," she said.

That was easy; I thought back on my own life often. "As far as I can recall," I told her, "there was really nothing remarkable about my childhood. My mother has told me that I was a preemie and spent a couple of days in an incubator after birth. The social worker noted it on her pad.

"I recall that when I was ten years old I was chubby. I wasn't grossly obese, just fat enough to have my mother nag at me to cut down on desserts and snacks a bit. I didn't. Instead, I continued asking for generous portions of Mother's homemade pies and ice cream, and got them.

"I am an only child and always wished I had brothers and sisters. I felt that my parents loved me, but they had problems getting along with each other, which used to upset me. I can remember that I used to cry after hearing my parents quarreling loudly. My grandparents absolutely spoiled me. I liked school and was a good student. In the main I think I was satisfied with life at that time.''

"When I was seventeen I had a girlfriend, Trudy, who talked incessantly about wanting to become a fashion model. Several times I went to fashion shows with Trudy and her mom. As I watched the slim models showing off elegant new fashions I wished more than anything to become as slim and fashionable as they were. I shared this wish with my mother, but she only tried to discourage me. I felt that Mom just didn't want me to grow up. She wanted me to remain her chubby little ten-year-old girl. That's when she found out how stubborn I could be.''

"She found then how stubborn you could be?'' The social worker echoed.

I nodded. "For a long time I've hated my looks. 'You're too fat! You've got to lose weight!' '' I would tell myself in a mirror. Dieting became all important to me. In some strange way, I felt that by not eating I was punishing myself for being the kind of person I was.''

The little social worker looked up at me for a moment, then continued writing her notes on what I had said.

"While I attended junior college,'' I continued, "I tried various diets and had an exercise program of running two miles before classes. I did push-ups and sit-ups in the evening trying to keep my weight down. I had a scale in my room and as soon as I gained any weight I would take laxatives and increase my exercising even more. Mom tried to talk me out of dieting. She wanted me to see a counselor and get professional help, but I refused. I didn't want anyone to find out that I had another me inside of the usual me.''

''Another you?'' the social worker asked me.

''It seems as if every few days another me—a different person—takes control. This person is much stronger than the usual me. This superstrong person, somehow, breaks my will to stay on my diet. It seems hard to explain,'' I said, feeling helpless. ''It's as if this other person scoops something vital out of my stomach, leaving me feeling hollow and empty inside. I'm afraid, then, that unless I immediately replace what has been taken out, terrible things will happen to me.''

I stopped. I realized that it was the first time I had shared this secret with anyone. I frowned at the tiny social worker. I didn't really want to talk about these strange personal feelings with her. ''I think I'm crazy,'' I said after a while, taking a deep breath.

''People who think they're crazy, seldom are,'' the social worker replied. ''People who are really crazy seldom doubt their sanity." I thought that over.

"In what way does this superstrong person manage to make you break your diet?" she asked, returning to the subject.

"While in college I used to order a couple of pizzas every four or five days, lock myself in the bathroom, and wolf them down, hardly even tasting them. At other times, it might be ice cream, cake, cookies, or candy I bought at the supermarket. After I gulped all the food down, I'd feel stuffed as a balloon that's too full and ready to burst. I was always angry at myself then and had an overwhelming urge to undo my bingeing."

"So you purged yourself." I felt that the social worker understood.

"I still do," I told her. "I put two fingers of my right hand deep into my throat, press down hard on the back of my tongue, take a deep breath, tighten my stomach muscles, and heave up most of the food. Then I can laugh at the superstrong person who made me break my diet. 'Ha! Ha! I won,' I taunt her, but I know now that the superstrong person will always come back."

"And this still happens?"

"In the shopping center near the apartment where I now live, a Mrs. Kreigmann opened a

Viennese pastry shop last year. She does her own baking and is very generous with the whipped cream. I'm a regular customer and she keeps asking me how my children are. She thinks I am buying desserts for a family of six.''

''And the scenario is the same?''

''The same,'' I said, beginning to feel that I had been talking for a long time. ''Only it's Mrs. Kreigmann's creations now instead of the pizzas and ice cream of a few years ago.''

I wished that the interview were over. The social worker must have sensed it.

''There are some questions I need to ask you, but we'll leave them for another time,'' she said, closing her pad. ''In the morning you are scheduled to see Dr. Grant, our psychologist. You will also have weekly appointments with our psychiatrist, Dr. Mira Falk. Even though she may not see you between appointments, she will be monitoring your progress from the daily reports she receives from other staff members. She'll see you more frequently if she thinks it's necessary. Mrs. Cortez is the social worker who will be available to you at any time. Your evaluation will include brain chemistry and hormone balance tests. Medication may be prescribed.''

Bulimarexic patients eat in a special dining room, dubbed by our predecessors ''the Shrine.'' The room had light yellow walls trimmed with a colorful floral border. There was always a tablecloth and fresh flowers on the table. Barely audible, pleasant background music could be heard if one stopped to listen.

I sat across from Stephanie and admired her large dark eyes set in her full, round face. I marvelled that anyone who looked so well-fed could be a bulimia patient—unless, of course, her purging had been unsuccessful. Mildred, on the other hand, with straggly blonde hair and pale blue eyes looked like some aesthetic commune's castoff as she sat at the table expressionless. Olga was her usual outgoing self. Edward, an upbeat athletic-looking member of the staff, ate dinner with us every evening. He was supposed to be our role model and had, what seemed to us, an astounding appetite. Among ourselves we called him the "vulture."

At breakfasts and luncheons he was replaced by Mary Spencer, whose long dark hair was tied into a neat bun nestling on the back of her head. Mary told us to imagine a pleasant experience we'd had in life. She suggested that we try to imagine that with each mouthful the experience became even more pleasant and satisfying.

Mildred claimed that she couldn't recall any pleasant experiences. Mary then suggested that she imagine that someone she didn't like stood over her and ordered her *not* to eat the food on her plate. Amazingly, Mildred started picking at the food with her fork when she imagined this. After a while she'd eat what she at first said she couldn't.

It seemed to us that Mary, like Ed, had a remarkably good appetite. It struck us as odd that neither of them was obese considering the large amount of food they consumed. Were they purging, I wondered. I quickly dismissed this unfair suspicion.

We were kept so busy it seemed we hardly had time to think of things that used to occupy our minds before we started the program. It was like being back in school taking an overload. In a way it was really like being in school because staff members taught scheduled classes. One of these was assertiveness training. There we acted out situations where we stood up for our rights. Mildred, Stephanie, and I felt we needed it. But all Olga had to do was to act her natural self. In another class we were taught relaxation techniques and had to practice them every evening.

The staff told us to do the very best we could in our classes on impulse control since they were extremely important. I found them difficult. It was hard to be tying knots or folding papers and then, when a buzzer sounded, stop immediately. I always felt a strong need to check my work more often than the others to try to make absolutely certain that I'd done everything just right. At the bank they used to call me a perfectionist.

There was a class in the program where we acted out situations, like in a play—"psychodrama," the staff called it. We were taught to try to overcome our compulsions to be perfect in everything we did. We had to practice giving ourselves silent mind signals to interrupt what we had started to do, such as smiling, frowning, running, or dropping a ball we had in our hand ready to throw. We practiced dismissing thoughts that happened to be in our minds and substitute other thoughts.

The classes I liked most were taught by an enthusiastic, bouncy lady who was an associate professor of medical anthropology at the local university. We learned that in some cultures obesity is viewed favorably. She showed slides of the Banyankole people in East Africa who fatten their young women and restrict their exercise from age eight in order to prepare them for marriage.

"But we're living in the USA!" Olga interrupted.

The professor smiled. "There are changing fashions in what is desirable appearance even in our country. The starved-looking model wasn't always popular here. In the early part of this century, the well-padded 'Gibson Girl' was the ideal of womanhood in the United States. Who knows," the professor said, shrugging, "the dieting programs all over the United States may some day convert to fattening programs if it becomes fashionable again to be plump."

A nutritionist described the 'set point' everyone is born with that controls one's weight, and she showed us charts illustrating the futility of ignoring one's natural 'set point' when dieting. I had not expected to get dancing lessons, but interpretive dancing was scheduled a couple of times a week. In the dancing class we had to try to translate our feelings into body movements. Everyone was clumsy at first, and hardly moved. After a while, we loosened up. It must have been hilarious to watch us. We all had a good laugh at ourselves.

In our evening group therapy sessions, presided over by a nurse-therapist, we discussed how we had related to the day's events. The therapist let us do most of the talking and usually only summarized what we had said. Every few days a volunteer, who had been a former patient in the program, came to our group sessions and listened to our discussions. She would point out when we used what she called 'denial.' She disarmed us by reminding us that she had gone through the same program and had used lots of denial herself. She urged us to support and encourage each other but, also, to be frank in criticizing ourselves and the others.

It seemed to me that Mildred got more than her share of criticism. "Why don't you get out of your shell?" Stephanie asked her once.

"What shell?" Mildred asked, clearly annoyed.

"What I mean is that you're always playing games! You play hide and seek with yourself. You don't seem to want to find your real self."

"Isn't that what we all have been doing?" I asked Stephanie. "Isn't our eating disorder really a hide-and-seek game that we've been playing with ourselves much of our lives? For years my weak self hid from a strong self that made me binge. After defeating the strong self by vomiting, it was the strong self's turn to hide."

"I'm not any worse than anyone else here!" Mildred announced more assertively than she would have before she entered the program. "Besides," she added, "I'm changing."

"I think that we're all changing," Olga observed. It was true. We had been warned against overconfidence, but, nevertheless, in some important ways we were now different from the persons we had been when we started the program.

On our last day, Dr. Falk informed us that we would continue getting therapy on an outpatient basis. She told us the program was ongoing and that the staff would always be available to us if we needed help to regain our controls.

As we filed out of the room we were each given an envelope containing a letter of congratulations from the director of the hospital. It contained a list of national and local organizations devoted to helping persons with eating disorders. To our surprise, there was also a letter of appreciation from the chef in charge of the hospital kitchen! He had dropped in on us once during our evening meal asking how we liked his cooking. With his ample girth and big smile he demonstrated that one can be both fat and happy.

After I had been back at work about a week or so, I was surprised when I looked up and saw Olga. She had come to the bank to open an account. We agreed to meet for dinner. No dieting and no bingeing, we promised each other. Ed and Mary would have been proud of us!

At dinner, Olga told me that she had heard that Sarah Bentley was a patient participating in the bulimia program we had just completed.

"Do you remember Sarah Bentley?" Olga asked me.

"No," I admitted after thinking a bit. "The name has a familiar ring though," I added, puzzled.

"She's the intake social worker at the hospital—the skinny blonde."

"I didn't catch her name when I was introduced to her," I said, stunned at the news. I pictured her in my mind. "There was something about her—I don't know just what—that made me feel she was anorexic or bulimic," I told Olga.

"I guess you've got to be one to know one," Olga said, shrugging.

"You'd think she would try to get help at a different facility than the one where she was an important member of the staff, wouldn't you?" I asked.

"It takes guts," Olga insisted. "If she's cured, she certainly will be an inspiration to future patients with eating disorders."

"And to former patients, too," I added.

## COMMENT:

*The hospital used cognitive-behavioral therapy in its eating-disorder program. This therapy has variations and provides for creative innovations. Basically, it consists of 're-educating' the patient's outlook on her/himself. Enjoying eating has to be 'rediscovered' and the patient must learn to view food as something positive. Training in impulse control is an important component of therapy.*

*Not all bulimia patients are emaciated. Persons of normal weight, and even some who are overweight, may have bulimia nervosa or bulimarexia as the disorder is called. It is dynamically related to another eating disorder, 'anorexia nervosa,' where* there is no bingeing and purging. Their etiology and thinking patterns toward weight and body shape are similar. There may even be crossovers of symptoms in these disorders, since some anorexic patients also have temporary bingeing periods. An eating disorder inventory is sometimes used to identify traits of perfectionism, oppositionalism, interpersonal distrust, lack of self-confidence, and a desire to retreat from the demands of adulthood. These are characteristics often observed among patients with bulimia and anorexia nervosa.

Ongoing research suggests that a specific brain hormone may play a contributory role in the development of bulimia. At one time eating disorders were ascribed exclusively to faulty child-mother relationships. With the new thinking accompanying the advances in neurophysiology, it is rare that any single factor can be held totally responsible for an emotional or behavioral disorder. Environmental influences, defects in the functioning of enzymes and neurotransmitters, genetic predisposition, foetal development, and hormone imbalance are among the factors that may combine in one way or another to create abnormal behavior. This does not invalidate the use of psychological treatment of behavioral disorders as in Melissa's case. It does, however, require a view of the total person in mental health evaluations. This was the goal of the eating disorder program in which Melissa participated.

It was the department's research policy to periodically assign a staff member to participate in the program to obtain an insider's view. Sarah Bentley

*was not bulimic. Thanks to her set point she re-
mained naturally thin.*

*An uncontrollable urge to steal things for which one has no need and can easily afford certainly deserves a place in any catalog of bizarre behaviors. Called kleptomania, the urge does not stem from hate, revenge, or a desire for excitement. The stolen items have no monetary or symbolic value to the person taking them. Actually, a kleptomaniac seems to gain nothing from stealing except a fear of ending up in jail. Or is there something we are overlooking?*

# KAREN:
# A Mysterious Urge

## THE FIRST VISIT:

Some of the pieces of the jigsaw puzzle that make up my life were placed into it upside down. I couldn't turn them right side up even after years of trying. That's why I found myself sitting in the psychiatrist's office on a beautiful, mild spring day last year.

The psychiatrist was a tall, slim man somewhere between thirty and forty. He had a neatly trimmed brown moustache and wore a blue sport jacket, light blue shirt, and a maroon tie.

"How can I help you?" the doctor asked smoothly. I remember thinking that he had a good professional manner. I decided to begin by telling him what I had done to try to help myself before I came to see him.

"I want to understand why I shoplift and have spent a lot of time reading books on abnormal behavior." I looked at him to see how he would take this.

"And how did that work out for you?" I couldn't detect the disapproval in his voice that I had expected for not seeking professional help earlier.

"I found that my symptoms match those of kleptomania. I steal things that I really don't want or need. I can't stop myself." I felt my jaw tightening as the psychiatrist picked up a pen and began to take notes.

"I have a college degree in English and work as a copywriter for *The Morning Herald*. It isn't easy to live in constant fear of being discovered and labeled a thief. They'd be shocked at the newspaper if that happened because I'm known there for having a high standard of ethics."

"How long have you had an urge to shoplift?" the psychiatrist asked.

"Since I was a teenager."

"And how often were you caught?"

"I usually get away with it. I guess I just don't look like a thief. I dress well and if I'm actually caught, I can quickly make up convincing explanations. Two weeks ago a salesgirl saw me slip a scarf into my purse and called the manager. He asked me to follow him to this office and then phoned the police. When the policeman came and questioned me, I showed him my newspaper employee ID card and told him I was writing a story on shoplifting. I said that I planned to pay for it on my way out. Neither one of them wanted any trouble with the newspaper. I gave the manager my check for the amount I owed, and they let me go. I don't think they were fooled though. I didn't sleep well that night."

The psychiatrist nodded, showing me he understood how I felt.

"What did you learn from trying to help yourself?"

"I learned that kleptomaniacs imagine that the things they steal are 'presents' that substitute for being loved. I guess if they had to be bought they couldn't represent love." I glanced at the psychiatrist. I saw no hint of his agreement with what I had said.

"Do you feel that you were deprived of love?"

"I don't know," I said, thinking it over. "I know my parents loved me, but they gave my younger brother many more privileges than they allowed me. I always thought that was unfair. Do you think that sibling rivalry played a role in causing my problem?"

The psychiatrist shrugged. ''At this point we can't tell.''

''After a while I became confused by the conflicting views on mental health that I came across. At one point I thought I shoplifted to express my repressed feelings. Then I read that emotional problems come mostly from unrealistic expectations and self-destructive habits. Another author wrote that rebelling against growing up led people to do foolish things without knowing why they did them. That seemed to fit me. An article I read a couple of months ago said that now researchers have found that inherited tendencies might be the reason.''

''Inherited tendencies?''

''My mother told me that I had a great-uncle who had what she called an 'affliction.' He used to wash his hands as many as forty times a day because he thought he was contaminated by things he touched. Is it possible that my compulsion to steal is a genetic defect that he and I share?''

''There would have to be more to it than that,'' the psychiatrist answered. ''Did you try to get help for your problem before you came to see me?'' he asked, changing the subject.

''I have always avoided confiding in anyone,'' I admitted, and then realized that I felt uncomfortable. ''But after my last close brush with the police, I decided to make an appointment to see you.'' I watched the psychiatrist taking notes on what I had said.

Something inside me loosened. Suddenly I heard myself blurting out, ''I don't know how much longer I can cope with having to steal!'' I pressed my lips together and held back tears. ''Do you think you can help me?''

''That depends largely on you,'' the tall man replied, looking straight at me. ''Less than five percent of arrested shoplifters are kleptomaniacs, but many more than that claim their stealing is caused by an uncontrollable impulse.''

For just a moment I wondered if he thought I might be one of those. I began to feel even more uneasy.

''People with impulse control disorders have been helped and some have been cured. However, other disorders with similar symptoms must first be ruled out,'' he continued.

It struck me that there might be something else wrong with me other than my self-diagnosed kleptomania. It was comforting to be in competent hands.

When the doctor asked, ''Do you want to tell me some events in your life that you feel were important?'' I knew then that the psychiatric session had begun in earnest.

''Every time I shoplift I feel that something

important is occurring in my life. It always seems mysterious because I don't steal to own the things I take. Sometimes I feel like I really want to be caught, but that doesn't make sense because I don't want to go to jail. After I got the job with the newspaper I was afraid that someone might find out about my shoplifting. Ever since I started there I have been afraid of being tagged a criminal and getting fired from my job.'' I rubbed my hands and found that my palms were moist. I hoped the psychiatrist could see that I was getting upset.

"I seem to be hooked on shoplifting like an addict is hooked on drugs," I complained. "While I am slipping something into my purse or tucking it into my clothing, tension seems to flow out of me and leave me calm. But the calm is soon replaced by another tension that comes from fear and self-hate.''

The doctor nodded his understanding. "Can you recall a period in your life when the impulse to shoplift was strongest?'' he asked, speaking more softly now.

"After my fouled-up love life," I replied, reluctant to think about it.

"Do you want to tell me something about that?''

I really didn't want to, but took a deep breath and went on. "My parents were religious people, and I was brought up to believe that sex was okay only after marriage. Three years ago I married a man I admired for his values. I respected Albert, a computer programmer I met at work, because he didn't try to get me into bed before we were married. After we were married, I realized he was impotent and incapable of sex.''

The psychiatrist's neutral grunt bothered me.

''I made him go for therapy, but it didn't work out. I think he wanted a mother instead of a wife. While I was married I felt a need to shoplift almost daily. After our divorce, a couple of months went by before I felt that need again.''

''I understand how that must have affected you,'' the psychiatrist said, picking up a small brass paperweight from his desk and stroking it. As the sessions continued, I noticed that he often did that. I wondered if that little act might be his own compulsion.

''Being 'good' is unrewarding,'' I said, thinking of my marriage and many other things that had happened in my life.

''Being good is unrewarding?'' he repeated lifting his eyebrows. I guessed he wanted me to tell him more about that.

''It seems that people who try to be good get into trouble more often than other people. The only thing I ever did wrong was shoplifting.

I admit that's pretty bad. If I had been less conforming when I was younger, would I ever have had a need to shoplift?''

''It's more complicated than that,'' the psychiatrist replied. ''If you want to go through with therapy, you'll have to decide whether you are willing to put in the necessary effort. You may have resistance and we'll have to overcome it. While in therapy you'll have to practice techniques for reducing the strength of your impulses and learn how to delay acting on them. You will have to practice substituting other activities for shoplifting, and this may require making changes in your life-style. There are some new medications that may be helpful as an adjunct to psychotherapy. However, your prognosis depends primarily on your commitment to make the required effort.''

Deep down I must have wanted to rid myself of my curse more desperately than I had realized. ''Yes, Doctor,'' I said, feeling tears again starting to fill my eyes. I'll do anything to be cured!'' I thought a moment then added, ''Or even just to be less tense and frightened.''

FINAL SESSION—Eight months later:

''Good morning, Dr. Hammond,'' I said, smiling as I took my seat facing him. The office had become a pleasant, comforting place during the eight months I'd been coming.

Dr. Hammond gave me a friendly nod. "Congratulations, Karen! You haven't had a relapse for months and you are doing great! This is the last of your four follow-up sessions."

I looked at him closely for signs of regret that I no longer would be seeing him. How silly of me, I thought. I'm not his only patient. Nevertheless, I was glad to hear him say, "Of course you know where to find me if that should become necessary."

Dr. Hammond consulted his notes. "In the last five months you have been able to control the impulse to shoplift. More important, during the last three months, you have felt no urge at all to steal."

It was true. At various times in my life, months and even years have passed in which I did no stealing. But the urge was always there waiting for a chance to spring out from within and force me to steal again. In the last three months I had tested myself over and over, walking through department stores as well as other kinds of stores. The dreaded urge was dead and gone. I was a different person.

Suddenly I shivered. I glanced at the thermostat on the wall across from where I was sitting. Dr. Hammond noticed it. "Excuse me," he said getting up and walking over to the thermostat. "It's chilly. I'll turn the heat up a bit."

After he adjusted the thermostat, he turned

around, grinning and said, "No need for you to be cold on your last visit here."

"He really is a caring person," I thought, as I had several times before.

"Probably I shouldn't ask this question," I said, looking at him carefully, "but is there any way you can tell whether I'm really cured?" I held my breath.

"Only time can tell if you have permanently gained the necessary impulse control," Dr. Hammond replied. I was sure he knew how much his answer meant to me.

"After your diagnostic evaluation and testing, we found that you really did have kleptomania. People with this disorder have been cured with the therapy you received. It is best if you think of yourself as cured."

I felt lucky. Everything that had happened since I had been seeing Dr. Hammond had worked out well. "Thank you for helping me, Dr. Hammond," I said, feeling warm gratitude. "My whole life has been changed for the better. When I first came to see you, I didn't believe it could happen. It seems too good to be true."

"You did the major part of the work," Dr. Hammond said as he leafed through my folder. "Your good motivation helped you overcome your initial resistance. Then, practicing redirecting your impulses gradually enabled you to gain control. Fortunately, you experienced no significant side effects from the medication I prescribed for you. I admit there were some ups and downs during the therapy,'' he said, glancing at me and smiling.

My psychiatrist stood up. It was time for me to leave. I swallowed a lump in my throat. ''Good-bye,'' I said. ''Thank you again.''

Dr. Hammond continued leafing through his notes after Karen had left his office. As he reached for his dictaphone to dictate the case summary, he noticed that his brass paperweight wasn't in its usual place on his desk. He was sure he had seen it there that morning. He thought perhaps he had absentmindedly put it into a drawer sometime during the day. Frowning, he searched through the drawers, but did not find it.

He shrugged. It had no real value, but it was annoying. *It had no value*, he thought again, his eyes narrowing. But when could Karen have taken it? Then he recalled hearing a soft rustling sound behind him while he was adjusting the thermostat.

## COMMENT:

*Kleptomania is a relatively rare disorder, but it has gained attention because its unusual symptoms* may be found among people who are educated and financially well-off. There are several distinguishing characteristics that set kleptomania apart from ordinary stealing and other disorders in which stealing occurs. Stealing occurs in malingering, conduct disorder, antisocial personality, manic episode, and in schizophrenia. In organic brain disorder, forgetting that objects were taken may simulate kleptomania.

A specific cause of kleptomania has not been established, but the disorder has been associated with emotional immaturity that may exist even among intelligent people who have achieved vocational success. Environmental factors and personality defects are known to contribute to the development of impulse control disorders.

As mentioned earlier, researchers are taking a closer look at brain chemistry and neurotransmitters, such as serotonin, for clues to understanding abnormal behavior. However, most agree that environmental experiences are the chief factors leading to emotional maladjustment although they may not be the only ones.

What can be said about Karen's theft of her psychiatrist's paperweight? Was it done on the spur of the moment while his back was turned, or was it premeditated? Was her shiver genuine or contrived to give her the opportunity to steal the paperweight? What does the act suggest about her prognosis? Does it mean that her therapy was unsuccessful? Was there a symbolic aspect to the theft of the paperweight, or was the theft merely a token of her last goodbye to her former self—a sentimental souvenir, so to speak? Only time will tell.

*It can be hazardous to interrupt anyone who is in the act of making a momentous decision, even if it happens to be a fourteen-year-old girl. One never knows what a person may do. They may go so far as to kill whoever is interrupting them. Once some-one has a finger on the trigger of a gun and is determined to pull it, you may not live long if you interfere. And it doesn't matter who you are!*

# MICHELLE:
# Why Didn't I Kill Mom?

My name is Michelle. I think that the most terrible thing that can happen to a person happened to me. I have often thought back on it—even when I didn't want to. I'll explain, but first, let me tell you something about my family. Then I'll tell you what happened.

My sister, Lucy, is six years older than me. I also have a brother, John, who is four years older. Because my sister and brother are so much older, I often felt like I was an only child.

I remember how Mom and Lucy used to talk about clothes and things that didn't interest me. John and Dad were crazy about sports. They spent evenings sitting together watching sports on TV. Every weekend they went off to play racketball. I felt very lonely in those days. I used to wish I had a twin sister my age who would do things with me and who'd always be there for me to talk to.

It seemed that Grandpa was the only one who liked to spend time with me. He used to tell me about what his life was like when he was a boy. I loved to listen to Grandpa's stories. When he died, I felt like I lost my best friend.

The dream I had the week Grandpa died didn't make sense to me. I dreamed that I was an astronaut in a spaceship headed for Mars. It never got there because the spaceship crashed soon after takeoff. When I told Mom about my dream, she said it came from watching TV before going to bed. She didn't know that I hadn't watched TV all that week.

I didn't like telling Mom things that happened to me because I didn't think she really listened. She always had lots of things on her mind, like her volunteer work at the hospital and going shopping with Lucy. My teacher told Mom that my school work was going downhill in spite of the extra help she was giving me after school. Mom thought that maybe I was lazy. Dad said that my problem was that I wasn't as well organized as John and Lucy were. I didn't tell them that I really hated school and couldn't keep my mind from wandering when the teachers were talking.

One day Mom asked me if I had trouble hearing. I didn't listen to what she was saying when my mind was on other things, but she thought that I couldn't hear her words. I went for a hearing test and the doctor said I could hear fine. "Ah," Mom said after we left the doctor's office. "You *can* hear if you *want* to!"

In those days, Lucy was forever complaining that I was not doing my fair share of chores at home. Mom agreed with her. Several times I wasn't allowed to go to the movies with my friend, Mary, because I hadn't cleaned up my room after Mom told me to. More than anything I wanted my next birthday present to be a cat, but I couldn't have one because Lucy was allergic. When I looked at my face in the mirror and saw the pimples near my nose, I knew that I was not even the least bit pretty. It seemed that nothing in my life worked out right. Sometimes I wondered if it was all my own fault, and then I really began to hate myself.

We were together one evening in the family room while the news was on TV. John and I were doing homework. I wasn't paying much attention till Mom said, "What a tragedy!"

I looked up at the screen and saw a bus lying on its side with the metal all twisted up. Men were carrying some injured people to an ambulance. I also saw a dead person covered by a white sheet being carried away on a stretcher. It looked like someone about my size. I wondered what kind of a life she had before the accident. Somehow I thought it must have been pretty much like mine. I tried to imagine that I was dead and had become a ghost. Then my mind drifted off in a kind of daydream and I saw myself returning home as a ghost dressed in a white sheet.

Things changed for me for a while when a boy everyone called ''Bing'' was assigned to the seat next to me in school. We started talking and laughing together at funny things that happened in class, like the teacher dropped her chalk three times when she was trying to write on the blackboard. We'd talk about some of the other kids and complain to each other about our parents. Mom even asked me a few weeks later, ''Michelle, what has happened? You are like a different person these days!''

''She's found herself a boyfriend, Mom,'' Lucy said, smiling at the idea that Mom hadn't thought of it herself. ''Haven't you noticed how often Michelle looks in the mirror lately?'' She turned to me and asked, ''What did Mary say when she found out you had a boyfriend? She's supposed to do pretty well in that department herself according to her sister.'' Lucy was friends with Mary's older sister.

Mary was the only friend I had. From time to time we spent evenings together listening to tapes, talking, and watching our favorite TV shows. One day she saw me talking to Bing during lunch break. After school she said that she had never seen anyone with a nose as big as Bing's. "Have you ever noticed that he walks like a cat?" she asked me. The next day I saw her waiting around after school till Bing showed up. Then I saw him walk her home.

Right after that, Bing became Mary's boyfriend and they didn't want to have much to do with me. "I don't care!" I told myself. Let her have him! I don't want a guy with a big nose who walks like a cat!" I cried myself to sleep that night.

I remember the morning Mom asked me to get the newspaper from the driveway. I don't know why I unfolded the paper and glanced at the headlines. I usually wasn't interested in reading newspapers. A headline on the bottom of the front page caught my eye. It read, "TWO TEENAGERS DIE TOGETHER IN SUICIDE PACT."

The article said that a boy and a girl, both in the eighth grade, killed themselves for reasons no one could understand. Everyone who knew them was shocked. Their parents said that they had always been close friends and seemed very happy. But a girl who had been one of their best friends told the reporter that she knew that they had quarreled and had really been unhappy.

"They're not unhappy now," I thought. I reread the story to find out how they killed themselves. It said that they were found dead in the garage of one of their homes. They had started the car parked there and inhaled fumes from the exhaust pipe. Suddenly I knew what I was going to do to put an end to all my troubles. Relief flooded through me, but there was also fear. I decided that I would kill myself the same way they had.

I folded the paper and replaced the rubber band. When I took it in and handed it to Mom, she asked, "What took you so long? I thought you were helping the boy deliver his papers to the rest of the neighbors."

She unfolded the paper and glanced at the headlines like she usually did. A frown appeared across her forehead. I thought she was probably reading the headline about higher taxes. She sat down and kept reading. After a while she turned to me and gave me a long look. Then she said in a gentle voice I hadn't heard her use before, "I've been worried about you, Michelle. I must talk to your father about it." I wondered what Mom wanted to talk to Dad about.

I have often watched Mom start the car. I've even started it for her a couple of times myself. I figured that I could take the car keys out of her purse, start the car, keep it running, jump out, hold my nose and put my mouth right next to the exhaust. But when I pictured it in my mind, I decided I didn't want to die that way. It would take too long. I might change my mind before I was dead and then everyone would laugh at me. Besides, I hate the smell of gas fumes.

I had a cousin who killed herself by taking a whole bottle of sleeping pills. That would be a better way. When Grandpa was alive, there were lots of pills around. He needed them for his heart. But I didn't think there was anything in the house now that I could use.

At breakfast one morning, John and Dad were talking about the robbery that had happened at a house further down our street. John said, "They got away with the stereo, a TV set, jewelry, and all the cash that was in the house. They tied the people up and stuffed rags into their mouths so they couldn't call the police right away."

"It won't happen here," Dad said looking at John as if they shared a secret.

"Why won't it happen here?" Lucy asked Dad.

John gave Dad a knowing look and told her, "If any robber comes into our house, he'll be carried out covered by a white sheet."

"A white sheet—a white sheet," the words

kept echoing through my mind. I thought of the bus accident I'd seen on TV. Again, I imagined myself dead and being carried away under a white sheet, with Dad, Mom, John, Lucy, my teacher, Mary, and Bing standing around me crying.

At last I knew how I was going to kill myself. Dad kept a gun on the top shelf of the master bedroom closet. Once Lucy had seen the gun there while she was helping Mom clean house. She told me that the gun had bullets in it. I knew that my unhappiness would soon be over.

A couple of weeks after John and Dad had talked about the robbery, my parents left to go over to my Aunt Gertrude's house. She was over eighty and lived alone. She had phoned and asked my parents to come over to help her fill out some forms for Medicare.

I wondered why Mom kept asking me if I was feeling okay before she and Dad left. I hadn't been sick or anything and she couldn't know that I was planning to kill myself as soon as they left. I wanted to get it over with quickly. When my parents finally drove off, I checked to see what John and Lucy were doing. Lucy had her head bent over her homework, as usual, and John was watching a ball game on TV. I tiptoed upstairs to my parents' bedroom. I tried to be calm, but my heart was racing. It was getting dark, but I didn't turn on any lights. I wanted everything to happen in the dark.

I switched on the small flashlight I had brought with me and got up on a chair to look for the gun on the closet shelf where Lucy told me she had seen it. My hand moved back and forth under the blankets and between them. There was no gun! My hands were trembling and panic began to build up in me. I looked on the other shelves in the closet. The gun wasn't there.

I opened several dresser drawers and felt around among the things in there. I couldn't find the gun. Then I looked under the bed. There was a shoe box pushed way back where you wouldn't see it if you weren't looking for it. Why would Dad keep a pair of shoes in a box under the bed when all of his other shoes were very neatly lined up in the closet? I slid the box out from under the bed. I held my breath, but couldn't stop my hands from shaking as I took the cover off the shoe box. It looked like there was only some tissue paper and a pair of shoes in the box, but I could tell from the weight of it that there must be something else in there. I pushed my hand under the paper and struck something hard. It was the gun! It was heavy in my hand. My arms felt like they were attached to strings which somebody else was pulling. They seemed to move like a puppet's arms.

As I held the gun in my hand, I wondered where to aim it so it wouldn't hurt too much when I shot myself. I thought it would probably be best to put the bullet right through my head. Strings seemed to raise my arms. Cold metal touched my head. I felt my fingers tense on the trigger when suddenly the bedroom door opened. It flashed through my mind that my parents may have guessed what I was planning to do and came back to check on me. The next thing I knew, I saw Dad sprinting toward me. He looked like a wild animal about to attack! I pointed the gun at him and it went off.

How long has it been since I killed my father? I couldn't tell you. Time in the hospital sometimes goes very fast and sometimes slow, but never like it really does on the outside. I could be a psychiatrist myself with all the treatment I've received over the years that I've been here.

A couple of things are clear to me now. I used to think that I loved Grandpa. It was hard at first for me to accept the idea that I was really angry at him for dying when I needed him. I wanted to love Dad, but he didn't care much about me. He was mostly interested in doing things with John, and John always treated me as if I weren't important. When Bing left me for Mary, that was the final straw. All those who had hurt me were males. That's why I killed my father when I had my finger on the trigger of his gun.

I know that I must continue to work out my hatred of males before I will be allowed to go home to live with Mother. Where else would I go? John is somewhere in South America. Lucy and her family live far from home. Mother is pretty old by now and needs my help in keeping up the house. All I can think of is that I want to leave this hospital and go back to live with her. But to tell the truth I always liked Dad better. How lucky it was for Mom that she wasn't the first to come through the bedroom door that night.

## COMMENT:

*The law of parsimony is easy to understand. It maintains that simple explanations should be considered before complicated ones.*

*Taking her case history into account, the simplest explanation of why Michelle shot her father is that he ran toward her while she was in a state of high tension and holding a lethal weapon in her hand. Anyone startling someone so occupied risks losing his life. At some time or other Michelle got the idea that she hated males. I have seen mental patients, particularly hospitalized teenagers, accept their fellow patients' explanations of the cause of their problems or adopt false self-diagnoses while brushing aside those of the psychiatric staff. Teenagers who wish to call attention to themselves may wear their newfound insights proudly like new, stylish clothing.*

*The wish to call attention to oneself may be a factor in how suicide is committed. Some choose to die spectacularly by jumping from a bridge or from a roof or a tall building. Others want to leave behind an indelible message—"I told you so!" In Michelle's case, "Aren't you sorry now?"*

*Suicide is the third highest cause of death among teenaged children in the United States. Feelings of alienation, lack of self-worth, loss of a loved one, disappointment in a romantic affair, make some young people suicide-prone. Among older persons, illness, loss of a spouse, depression, loneliness, and displaced anger at another person have been identified as causes of suicide.*

*Signs that suggest a danger of suicide include: withdrawal from activities, a new carelessness in hygiene, silence or thoughtfulness not previously present, insomnia or excessive sleepiness, physical complaints, crying spells, poor appetite, loss of interest in what is happening.*

*Michelle's behavior was typical of a suicide-prone youngster. Her hospitalization was prolonged because she had difficulty in emotionally integrating what had happened. When she was finally discharged from the hospital, she went to stay with her mother. But mother and daughter didn't always get along well. Michelle admitted to herself that at those times she wished she had shot her mother instead of her father. Later, with follow-up counseling, she realized that she didn't hate her parents at all! She just couldn't tolerate interference.*

*Ralph was sure that his counselors would never figure out the real reason he kept setting fires. Nor would his mother, his teachers, nor the judge who sentenced him to Juvenile Hall discover it. How could they, when he hadn't told them the truth? He believed that only he could find the elusive cause for his compulsion because only he had all the facts. At first, Ralph's search led nowhere, but in the end he was sure he had found the source of the power the flames had over him.*

# RALPH:
# The Ghosts in the Flames

"He's the lowest little worm that crawls on earth," I heard one of the guards tell someone about me. The guard didn't know that I could hear him. My sharp ears have often helped me hear things that I wasn't supposed to hear.

"He's set four fires already," the guard told whoever he was talking to. "We're going to make sure he doesn't set another one!"

It scared me that the guard was talking about me like that, but it also made me feel kind of proud. There's not many kids my age in town as well-known to the cops as I am.

The counselors I've been sent to told Mom I

don't set fires just because I'm bored or trying to have fun like she thought. They told her that there was a deeper reason. I'm only a boy, but I know myself better than any counselor knows me. All the counselors know is what I tell them when they ask me questions. But how could they know what's inside of my head when I never tell them the truth about myself? If the real reason for my wanting to set fires is ever found, it'll be me who'll find it.

Since I was doing nothing while I was locked up in the small room in the Juvenile Hall detention building, I had plenty of time to think. I pretended that I was a detective looking back into my life to search for clues that would lead me to the real reason I want to set fires. I felt pretty sure I'd be able to discover it. Then I'll tell the counselors what it is. They'll be mighty sore that they hadn't been able to find it themselves. I'd have a good laugh at them then!

When I think back about things that have happened to me, the first memory that comes into to my mind is the time one of my teachers took me to see the school counselor. The counselor was a tall, skinny woman who tried to act friendly, but I could see that she really didn't mean it. I'd seen her type before and I didn't trust her. She asked me lots of questions. I didn't give her any right answers. Later, the counselor asked Mom to come to school to talk about me. Mom was always tired from having to work at two jobs, and she said I was causing her nothing but trouble.

Mom told me that the school counselor said that my "hostility" made me set fires. "Ralph is angry deep inside," she told Mom and explained that I wanted to punish the world for whatever the world had done to me. The school counselor told Mom that I should see a psychologist because I needed more help than she could give me.

I didn't see how the school counselor could tell Mom what went on "deep inside" of me when I hadn't told her the truth about any of the things she had asked me. Why did she tell Mom to take me to a psychologist when I had already seen the psychologists the judge made me go to? Mom knew that counseling from psychologists hadn't stopped me from setting fires. That's why Mom told me that what I needed more than psychologists was a good belting on my tail, and she promised to give me one that I'd remember the rest of my life.

I'm sure that the school counselor was wrong about my being angry at the world. Thinking that I'm angry when I set fires shows how little the psychologists know about what is really going on in my head. When I set fires I don't think about the world and I'm not angry. I feel happy and excited. All I think about when I set a fire is the fire engines coming with their sirens screaming.

I remember the last psychologist I went to. He asked me to do puzzles and play games with him. He showed me cards with pictures of people, and I had to guess what they were doing. None of it made sense to me, and I didn't try very hard to do what he asked. After I had answered a lot of questions, I got bored and said the first thing that came to my mind without even thinking. But he wrote down everything on his pad as if he believed that I meant it all.

At my hearing I sat next to a guy who the court had appointed to be my lawyer to make sure that I got my rights. There was also a psychologist, a social worker, my probation officer, a policeman, and Mom there. The people who were going to testify raised their right hands and swore to tell the truth about me. They talked about me and used big words I didn't understand. When they got through, the judge agreed the words they used fit me. It scared me to think that I've got some strange medical thing wrong with me. I guess it means that I'll never stop setting fires. I suppose when I'm eighteen I'll be sent to a big prison and have to stay there forever.

I was just a baby when my oldest brother joined the Navy and my other brother left home to work somewhere in another state. It's been years since I saw them. I was the youngest of five kids. When I was still small Mom told me that she hadn't wanted me because she couldn't afford to have another child. Sometimes I think she hates me for having been born. After working at the motel and then going to her other job cleaning people's houses, Mom is too tired to pay much attention to me. I guess that's why she never scolds my sisters for teasing me. I used to hope that Mom would stop them from calling me ''stupid,'' which was their favorite name for me. When she heard me cry because my sisters were teasing me, she yelled at me for making too much noise.

I don't know if hating school has anything to do with my wanting to start fires. I remember one day at school when I was daydreaming, as usual, to pass the time, my teacher asked me to tell the class what she had just finished explaining. I couldn't repeat a word of what she had said. Soon after that I was placed in special classes for dumb kids. There they used lots of pictures to teach us, but that didn't make me like school any better.

I wonder if being dumb in school is why I always get caught when I set fires. Some kids at school used to brag about how they stole money to buy dope to give them a high. Today those kids are still jacking around outside while I'm here in Juvy wondering why they got away with what they did and I got busted.

One thing that I always remembered was the little red fire engine Mom gave me for my birthday a long time ago when I was three or four. Mom was always complaining to my sisters and me that we were short of money. That's why I thought she must love me a lot since she bought that fire engine for me. The fire engine was one thing Mom wouldn't let my sisters take away from me. They tried a couple of times, and when I told Mom, she yelled at them that it was my birthday present. I didn't let that fire engine out of my sight. When I wasn't playing with it I kept it hidden in a place where no one but me could find it.

I remember one day when real fire engines raced past our house with their sirens screaming. They looked like my toy fire engine all grown up. The sound of the sirens made me excited. I wanted to run after them to see where the fire was. I knew I couldn't, so I played like my toy fire engine was one of the real ones that had raced past our house. I pushed my fire engine under Mom's chair and pretended that that's where the fire was. I sure was glad that Mom had bought me my toy fire engine.

Once when I was still pretty small, I found a box of matches in the kitchen drawer. I took out a match and struck it against the side of the box. Then I pretended I was lighting a cigarette with it, like Mom's friend did when he used to come over. When the flame started creeping toward my fingers, I got scared and threw the burning match into the brown paper bag where we put the garbage. The bag caught on fire right away, and the smoke made my eyes sting. I yelled for Mom. She came running into the kitchen, filled a pitcher with water, and poured the water on the burning bag.

After the fire was out, the garbage in the bag still smoldered. I remember how upset Mom looked as she scooped it into the dustpan and took it outside. The kitchen was a mess. Smoke was hanging in the air, and ashes and water were all over the floor. When Mom caught her breath, she turned me over her knee and gave me the hardest licking I ever got in my life. She said that she hoped that would teach me never to set things on fire again.

Sometime later when I was playing outside, something made me want to know how fast the grass would burn. I went into the house and took some matches from the kitchen drawer where I knew Mom had hidden them under some folded napkins. When I got back outside, I lit three matches and dropped them on the dry grass. I knelt down to shield the little flames that started up when the wind blew. I hardly heard my sister, Debbie, come running from the house screaming at me as she put the fire out. She said, ''Wait until I tell Mom what you did!''

In my mind I can still see Mom's face getting red when she found out that I had set another fire. While she was beating me she yelled, "If you ever play with matches again I'll kill you!" But I knew she wouldn't kill me because then she'd have to go to jail, and she couldn't work at the motel any more.

Since I still hadn't figured out what makes me set fires, I kept on thinking. I remember another fire I set by lighting a crumpled piece of newspaper and pushing it through the window of an empty house. I used to pass the house on my way home from school, and there was something about that house I didn't like.

Even before I could run away from the house I heard a crackling sound telling me that something inside had caught on fire. I remember running away faster than I'd ever run before. Out of breath, I stopped on a little hill a couple of blocks away. From there, I watched the growing orange brightness in the window where I had thrown the burning paper. Black smoke started coming out of it. Soon, I could see brightness in other windows. I watched the flames bursting out here and there all over the house, and wondered when the fire engines were coming.

It wasn't long before I heard them. I hoped that I'd soon see fire fighters jumping out of fire engines. But to my surprise, one of the sirens suddenly stopped right where I was standing.

Two cops jumped out of their car and grabbed me before I could run away. I still don't know how those cops found me so fast or how they knew that it was me who had set the fire. Once more I was in Juvy waiting for the judge to decide what to do with me.

From Juvy I was sent to a special boarding school that was pretty far away from home. Kids who had big problems were sent there to get the help they couldn't get anywhere else. We slept, ate, and went to classes all in the same building. The counselors who worked with us spent a lot of time teaching us how to understand ourselves. They said that self-understanding could show us what went wrong in our lives and would help us stop doing the things that got us into trouble.

I liked the counselors, but I didn't always tell them the truth when they asked me questions. While I was at the boarding school, setting fires didn't much enter my mind except once or twice. After a while, the people in charge decided that I understood myself well enough to go home provided I had follow-ups there. I remember how good I felt when Mom hugged me and welcomed me home. I never loved her as much as I did then. I didn't want her to be unhappy, and made up my mind never to set fires again.

There were people inside the house I set on

fire a couple of months later. I didn't know that at the time I broke a basement window and threw burning paper inside. The fire spread quickly inside the house, and it wasn't long before I saw people running out of a door carrying things. Again, I was surprised at how fast the police found me and picked me up. They brought me back to Juvy where I sat thinking about the flames that had leaped out of the windows of the house. In my mind, I could see the flames dancing, reaching upward. It seemed like they might take me with them, and something made me want to go. Suddenly it hit me that the flames themselves were the clue I had been looking for!

As I thought about flames, the answer to why I set fires came to me. I knew that it must be the right answer. The reason I keep wanting to set fires is because I was born with ghosts of unborn flames in my head! As I think about it, I can sometimes hear the ghosts, imprisoned inside of me, begging me to help them escape so that they can live. I have to help them live because they are a part of me. If I don't, that part of me will die.

I know that soon new counselors will ask me questions and try again to find out why I keep setting fires. But I won't tell them the reason that I figured out. I'm sure they'd laugh and wouldn't believe me. Since I now understand why I set fires, I'm sure that I'll probably keep on doing it. The ghosts of the flames locked up in my head will keep reminding me that they want to escape from within me. They want me to find them a house in which they can live.

## COMMENT:

*Ralph was unable to find an explanation he could accept for his need to set fires. Thus, his whimsical conclusion was not an altogether surprising one. Ralph is an emotionally immature youngster who rationalizes his behavior at his level of comprehension. Inadvertently, however, his fantasy of having been "born" with a compulsion brings to mind the perennial environment versus heredity issue.*

*The idea of a genetic component in shaping behavior is fraught with the great danger of oversimplification and misapplication. Genetic influences could apply only to a specific individual or close members of his family. No racial or ethnic generalization regarding genetically derived behavior can ever be scientifically justified because all humans share a common gene pool, and their behavioral traits are aligned along a curve of a normal distribution with standard deviations.*

*Most chronic arsonists tend to have difficulty in establishing satisfying interpersonal relationships. Inadequate and passive aggressive personalities are often found among them. Pathological lying, developmental delay, difficulty in thinking in the abstract are some common characteristic of young arsonists. In a structured environment, the tendency to set fires may disappear only to reappear again later upon return to the previous environment. Three Yale Psychologists writing in the* American Psychologist *(Aug. 1992) describe a number of programs that center on early childhood intervention and build on the strength of children's families as well as on the children themselves. The approach is broadly comprehensive and has been described in the article as "a promising preventative of juvenile delinquency." Had the various factors impacting on Ralph's life been integrated into an ongoing program of crime prevention, he might not have felt a need to find a house for the flames. Nor would he then have viewed flames as "locked up in his head."*

*Mom didn't expect her seven-year-old son, Jerry, and his younger sister, Cindy, to appreciate that she had divorced her husband mainly for their sake. But she did expect them to remain loyal to her. When she found them a new daddy, they asked to have their real daddy back. Things went from bad to worse. It seemed that their lives were starting to fall apart.*

# CINDY and ME: Mom's "Little Man"

Mom told Cindy and me that Daddy wasn't going to live at our house with us anymore. Cindy is three years younger than me. She asked Mom, "Why isn't Daddy going to live here anymore?" Mom said, "He wants . . . he has to . . . we are divorced now. It means that we now live our own lives without him." Mother smiled to show us that this was good.

Daddy had never paid much attention to Cindy and me except when he got mad at us. I was always a little afraid of him. If we didn't do things his way, he'd yell and sometimes spank us. I remember him pushing Cindy against the wall just because she was too slow in coming when he called her.

Sometimes after I was in bed, I used to hear Mom and Daddy yelling at each other. They sounded like they were awful mad. Once, late at night, when I got up to go to the bathroom, I heard Mom crying. I thought, "Daddy must have made her cry. I hate him!" I was glad that Daddy wasn't going to live with us anymore. I never wanted to see him again.

Mom hugged me and said, "You are going to be my little man now." Then she kissed me. Cindy looked at me with big eyes when Mom said that. Maybe she expected me to suddenly grow as tall as Daddy. I felt important but also a little scared. I didn't know what I'd have to do now that I was Mom's little man. I decided that I would hit anyone who tried to hurt her.

Mom used to hug me or pat my head when she reminded me that I was now her little man. Cindy watched Mom carefully when she said that. I felt it was very important that I do whatever a little man does. I didn't know what that was, but I hoped I wouldn't disappoint Mom.

Cindy followed me around a lot more than she did before Daddy moved out. She didn't fight with me as much and complain about me to Mom like she used to. Maybe she thought it would be wrong to fight with Mom's little man.

We drove over to the library one Saturday morning. Mom told Cindy and me that she wanted to look for a book that would help her understand children. I liked going to the library because it had lots of good books for kids. All around the outside of the library there was a park with grass and trees. There were always some men in old, worn-out clothes sleeping on the grass or just sitting on the benches. I looked to see if Daddy was one of them. I wondered if Cindy thought about where Daddy was sleeping now, since he didn't live with us anymore. But she didn't look at the men lying on the grass. She only wanted to be a baby and snuggle with Mom. I was sure that Mom was spoiling her.

My teacher wasn't spoiling me! I don't think she's as nice to me as she used to be. She told Mom that my mind wasn't on my schoolwork, and that my grades were slipping. Maybe I was thinking about too many other things. Sometimes I was thinking of what I could do to make Mom happy, and wondering where Daddy was now.

Mom surprised us one morning. She looked upset. She told us, ''Your father has asked to see you.'' At first I didn't understand what she meant. Cindy asked Mom, ''Are we going to visit Daddy?'' Mother said, ''Yes,'' and smiled to show us it would be okay. I thought it would be terrible to visit Daddy. I wouldn't know what to say to him. I was afraid he might beat me up if he found out that I was Mom's little man. My stomach felt like I was going to throw up. Cindy sang, "I'm going to see Daddy! I'm going to see Daddy!" Then she stopped and said, "I don't want to!" and started to cry.

Mom looked like she was going to cry, too. She hugged us and told us, "It won't be for long—just for the weekend. The time will go fast, and soon you'll be back home."

Cindy asked Mom, "What will Daddy look like? Where does he live? Why do we have to see him?"

"The judge ordered it," Mom told us, and it sounded like the judge was God, or maybe the devil. I don't know which one he was, but I could tell that if the judge ordered something, you couldn't say no. When I saw how scared Cindy looked, I decided I would protect her if Daddy hit her, even if he would beat me up afterwards.

It was a long drive to where Daddy lived. We started out early and didn't get there until the afternoon. Mom had to stop a couple of times to look at a map. At last we got there and found Daddy's apartment. We rang the bell. I couldn't believe that the man who opened the door was Daddy. He looked different from how I remembered him. He smiled at us and said, "Hi, kids—welcome aboard! We're going to have fun!" Then he patted me and Cindy on the head.

Mom and Daddy didn't say much to each

other. They just talked about what time Daddy would drive us back home on Sunday. I was glad that they didn't yell at each other like they used to when Daddy lived at home. I thought that getting divorced must be really good for people.

Daddy told Cindy and me, "This is a great day in my life!" He gave us presents—me a toy truck, and Cindy a little purse. He said that we could take them home with us so that we wouldn't forget him. I played with the truck, and Cindy took the purse and pretended she was shopping. Daddy said, "First we're going to a ball game and then we'll have a great dinner. You kids can have two desserts each!" Cindy didn't seem to be as afraid of Daddy as she thought she would be. I even saw her trying to snuggle up to him a little bit.

While Daddy was getting ready, the door bell rang and a tall lady came in. She was all dressed up and pretty, but not as pretty as Mom. When she saw us she smiled and said, "I've heard so much about you two." She turned to Daddy and said, "What lovely children you have!" She looked at Cindy and said, "Your little daughter is so cute!" and stretched the "so" to show she really meant it.

Daddy put his arm around the lady and said, "This is Ruth, kids. She's a great sport and a good friend. She's going to the game and out to dinner with us, and then she's going to stay and watch the late TV show after you kids are in bed.'' Daddy and Ruth looked at each other and smiled when he said that.

Watching the game was fun. After it was over, Daddy took us to a restaurant that had white tablecloths and candles on the tables, and everything looked pretty. A lady showed us where to sit, and after we sat down, Daddy let us order whatever we wanted. He said to the waitress, ''Tonight I'm celebrating the return of my kids to their rightful owner.'' The waitress said, ''How cute they are!'' Daddy replied, ''Yep, take right after their old man!'' Ruth laughed and said, ''And after his girlfriend!''

I thought that the food was the best I ever had, especially the chocolate cake with ice cream. There was lots of it and Cindy ate it all except for what fell on her best dress. Ruth told her not to worry because she'd wash it off when we got back to Daddy's house. When the waitress brought the bill, Daddy told us, ''I'm a very poor man and have no money. Be sure to tell that to your mother!'' He pointed to Ruth and said, ''I'd be starving if I didn't have this angel supporting me.''

After we got back to Daddy's place, he showed us a couch that unfolded to make a bed. ''I know you kids are tired after such a long day,'' he said, ''so, I'll let you go right to sleep.'' He waited until we were in bed. As he closed the door, he threw us each a kiss and said, ''Good night, sweethearts. I bet you're glad that you have such a good daddy.''

Next morning we were up before Daddy was. After a while he came into our room in his pajamas. His hair was mussed up and he was smoking a cigarette. With one hand he rubbed his eyes. ''I need my java!'' he told us in a sleepy voice.

I wondered what his java was and why he needed it. ''Come on kids, let's have breakfast,'' he said and led us to a little kitchen. He turned on a small TV in the kitchen and got milk and doughnuts for us, and made coffee for himself. While he was doing this he stretched and yawned saying, ''Life is rough, kids, life is rough!''

On the way home Daddy sang along with songs he played on his cassette player. He asked Cindy and me to sing with him. We didn't know the words and didn't want to. Later we just hummed the tunes while he sang, and it turned out to be fun. Cindy begged him to stop at a couple of ice cream places we passed along the way. He didn't seem to mind stopping. He didn't have any ice cream himself but was glad to buy it for us. I was surprised to see how much ice cream Cindy could eat. Daddy told her, "Don't get a stomachache or I'll get hell from your mother!"

When we got home, Daddy and Mom talked for a while. I could hear Mom say something about money, and saw Daddy shaking his head. When Daddy started to leave, he told Mom in a loud voice, "The kids had a great time with me. Don't spoil 'em!" Then he waved goodbye to Cindy and me and drove off.

After Daddy left, Mom put her arms around us and kept telling us, "I'm sure you're glad to be back home!" She gave me a special hug and told me, "I'm so happy to have my little man back." Then she asked us to tell her everything that happened at Daddy's house. We couldn't remember much except that we had a good time. Cindy showed Mom her purse and I showed her the truck Daddy gave me. That night Cindy asked me how long it would be before Mom would marry Daddy again.

Not long after our visit with Daddy, Mom told us that she had a friend she wanted Cindy and me to meet. She said it was very important for her to know if we liked him. A few days later, Joe, Mom's friend, came to our house.

Joe told us he had heard a lot about us. Right away he sat on the floor where Cindy was playing with her toys. He played with her until he saw a ball in her toy box. He picked it up and tossed it to me. We threw it back and forth across the room. He smiled a lot and I could see that he was trying to be our friend. Mom stood by watching and smiling, too.

It wasn't long after that visit that Mom told us that Joe was going to be our new dad. I told her I didn't want a new dad. I wanted my old dad—the one I had before Mom divorced him. Cindy didn't say anything, but I could tell that she was scared.

One day Mom got all dressed up and went out with Joe. When they got home, Mom told us that she and Joe had gone to the judge and gotten married. I could see that Mom looked very happy. But I thought that if the judge had married Mom to Joe, he was like the devil and not like God.

The next day Joe moved in with us. He brought all his clothes and things to our house. He said that he was our new dad now, and told Cindy and me to call him "Dad." He said that one of these days he planned to adopt us. He put his hands on both of our heads, but Cindy moved away from him. I wanted to, but I just stood there wishing he would go away. Cindy and I talked things over. We decided that we didn't want Joe to adopt us. We talked about running away from home. We hid some candy bars and cookies in the closet in my room to take along with us in case we did.

Whenever I saw Joe and Mom hugging and

kissing it made me mad! I felt like crying. I didn't think it was right for Mom to kiss and hug Joe. How could she do that after she told me that I was her little man? Cindy didn't say anything, but I knew she didn't want Joe to be her dad. I was sure that Mom could see that we didn't love Joe. One day she asked me, "Why do you keep calling your new father Joe instead of Dad?"

"His name is Joe and he's not my real father," I told her.

"He *is* your real dad in this house! If you visit your father at his house, you can call him 'Dad' too." She sounded angry.

"He's not my real dad!" I said, starting to cry. I wanted to ask her why she didn't call me her little man any more, but I didn't say anything. I began to think that maybe I didn't love Mom as much as I used to.

"Well, I'm not going to force you or your sister to call Joe 'Dad,'" Mom said, looking upset. "But your real father was mean to both of you. He never paid attention to you like Joe is trying to do. He didn't care for you. Joe is willing to adopt you if he can." She began to cry while she told us this.

I didn't say anything, but I knew that Cindy and me wanted our own daddy back. Cindy asked me if he would ever come back to live with us. I told her that I didn't think so. I wasn't Mom's little man any more, but I was Cindy's big man now.

After a while, Joe gave up trying to play with us. Sometimes he yelled at us for no good reason, just like Mom said our real daddy used to before Mom made him move out and divorced him.

Mom seemed different from the way she was before she and Joe got married. She didn't smile much anymore. Some days she looked upset the whole day. Once she told Cindy and me that we weren't even a little bit grateful that she left our daddy mostly because he was a rotten father. She said that Joe had been trying his best to be a good father to us, but we wouldn't let him.

I was sorry to see Mom so upset. I remembered how happy she had been when she first told us that Daddy wasn't going to live at home anymore. So I asked her why she didn't get divorced from Joe so that she would be happy again like she was after she divorced Daddy.


MOM

When, Jerry, my seven-year-old son, suggested that I divorce Joe, I had already made an appointment for family counseling. It seemed that our lives were starting to fall apart. Jerry was doing poorly in school, and Cindy had wet her bed several times. I was unable to hide from my children my disappointment over their unwillingness to accept Joe as their stepfather.

I was relieved when the counselor told us that our problem was not unusual. After a divorce and a new marriage, children often reject their stepparent and show an unexpected loyalty to their biological parent, even if their previous relationship with that parent had been poor. The counselor advised Joe to be patient and spend some individual time with Jerry and Cindy. He suggested that, for the time being, Joe leave the disciplining to me.

With the counselor's help, we learned how to communicate more effectively with the children, and in time were able to get them to respond to us without resentment. In the end, our situation turned out not to be the disaster I had feared. After a while, Jerry and Cindy saw that I could "be happy again" without having to get another divorce. But the children never called Joe "Daddy" and we didn't ask them to do so, even after Joe legally adopted them several years later. The children seemed to retain their loyalty to their biological father. I found it disturbing, but in time I learned to live with it as they had learned to live with Joe.

## COMMENT:

*It is not unusual for an adjustment disorder to follow in the wake of a divorce, especially when young children are involved. As often happens after a divorce, Mom had relied too heavily on her seven-year-old son for emotional support. He was unable to serve her need as an emotional replacement for her former spouse. Newly divorced parents may unwittingly give their children too much responsibility, as when they assign them adult roles.*

*Young children of recently divorced parents may have fears and anxieties after the parent who does not have custody leaves home. They may convert their anxiety into illnesses or behavioral changes such as doing poorly in school or losing interest in their former activities. These symptoms are often seen among children with adjustment disorders.*

*Court-ordered visits with the parent who does not have custody often confuses children, especially when this parent makes a special effort to convince them that he/she is a very nice person who shouldn't have been divorced. The experience may lead children to have conflicting loyalties and lose trust in the custodial parent. Matters are made worse when one of the divorced parents criticizes the absent parent in order to gain the children's sympathy.*

*Mom's new husband, Joe, had good intentions when he tried to win the children over, but he failed to realize that gaining acceptance as a stepfather takes time. Patience, flexibility, and experimentation are required. Family counseling before or after a divorce is often successful in helping the divorcing parent give up unrealistic expectations.*

*Stories are an excellent way to teach children about life. But one has to be aware that sometimes they don't do the job they are supposed to do, and that can lead to tragedy. In Alice's case, the problem might have been that good lions and bad lions really do look alike, especially when a magician has changed them into people. Alice was certain she could tell the difference.*

# ALICE:
# Never Go with a Stranger

My name is Alice and I am six years old. Last week while I was walking over to Judy's house—Judy is a year older than me—a blue shiny car stopped right where I was walking. A man all dressed up in a gray suit, white shirt, and a tie got out and came over to me smiling.

"I got a girl just like you at home," he said. "She's alone and wants someone to play with her. I have a nice chocolate candy bar in my car, and I'll give it to you to eat." He looked around and then opened the car door for me to get in, saying, "Jump in, hurry!"

I felt sorry for the little girl at the man's house who had no one to play with. I could play with Judy some other day, I thought. But just then

Judy came walking along on her way to my house. She planned for us to play with my new toy computer game I got for my birthday last month. When she saw me about to get into the car with the man, she yelled, "Alice! Don't go with him! Come with me. We're going to your house to play." I told her, "He promised to give me candy!" Judy pulled me away and the man got back into his car and quickly drove off.

When we got to my house, Judy told my mom that she had seen me about to get into a strange man's car. Mom got very upset when she heard this.

"You must never get into anyone's car!" she warned me.

"Not even in our car?" I asked.

"I don't mean that," Mom said. "Don't ever go anywhere with a stranger—someone you don't know."

"Why?" I asked.

"Because—because some people may be bad and want to hurt you."

"Why, if I didn't hurt them?"

"Because some people are sick in their mind and they might hurt little children for no reason."

"Are they in a hospital?"

"Never mind!" Mom said. "I'm telling you

never, ever, go with a stranger even if he prom-
ises you candy!''

''Is it okay if he doesn't promise me candy?''
I asked, thinking of the lonely girl in the man's
house who had no one to play with.

''Bad people don't tell you the truth. They
could be mean and may hurt little girls,'' Mom
said. ''They might take them away and never
let them come home again!''

''Not this man, Mom,'' I told her, knowing
she was wrong. ''He was smiling and
friendly.''

Mom didn't say anything more. She just went
to the telephone and called Grandma. Judy and
I played with my new toy computer game I got
for my birthday. She knew how to use it and I
didn't yet. But I pretended I was Dad and Judy
was me and I was teaching her how to use it,
even though she knew more about it than I did.

That evening Grandma came over to our
house. She talked with Mom and Dad for a
while and then she said she was going to tell
me a story about lions and a girl named Tammy.
Grandma knew that I loved to listen to her stories. I was glad she was going to tell me a story
about lions. Long ago she gave me a stuffed
lion and it still was my favorite toy. I slept with
it every night. Once when I saw some real lions
and their cubs on TV, I asked Mom to buy me
a live pet lion for Christmas.

Grandma took me to my room and sat next to me on my bed. She looked at me and smiled. "Well, here we are together," she said. "It is important that you listen very carefully to the story I am going to tell you."

"Once there was a little girl named Tammy. Tammy liked the lions she had seen in pictures in her books. So, she asked her grandmother to take her to a place where she could see real, live lions. One day she saw big signs all over town telling people that a circus was coming. Tammy's grandparents promised to take her to the circus where she would see the real, live lions. Tammy could hardly wait. At last the day came when her grandparents took her to the circus.

"At the circus Tammy saw clowns do somersaults, elephants dance, and a man walk on a wire high above the people's heads. At last she saw what she had been waiting for. She saw real, live lions in a ring behind a fence, running in a circle around a lady in shiny clothes wearing cowgirl boots. Tammy watched as some of the lions walked straight up on their hind legs and others jumped through hoops held by the lady—'the lion lady,' Tammy called her. The lions were having lots of fun. Tammy wished she could pet them and play with them.

"After the shows were over and people began to leave, Tammy asked her grandparents if they could take her to the lady who had put on the lion show.

" 'Oh lion lady,' Tammy said when they found her, 'please let me pet your real, live lions and play with them.'

"The lion lady frowned and said, 'Real, live lions aren't like people! They are wild animals with sharp claws and big teeth. Some lions are good and probably wouldn't hurt you. But other live lions are bad, and if you petted them they might scratch you or even bite you.' "

"Can you remember that, Alice?" Grandmother asked. "Some lions are bad and would hurt you!"

"Yes, Grandma," I said. "What happened after Tammy found that she couldn't pet the real, live lions?" I asked her.

"The next day Tammy went shopping at a mall with her parents. There she saw a crowd of children gathered around a magician who was just finishing a magic show. He said that he was going to do his last magic trick of the day. Tammy and her parents stopped to watch him.

"On the magician's table there was a large cloth-covered object. He pulled the cloth off and the children saw a bird cage. Inside the cage sat a red and green parrot, blinking its eyes. 'Oh, what a nice bird!' the children said, waiting to see what the magician would do next.

"The magician covered the cage again with the cloth. He told the children that he could change the parrot into any animal they wished.

" 'Please change it into a kitten,' Tammy called out.

"The magician turned to Tammy and told her, 'I'll ask you three questions to see what you really want. What happens to kittens when they grow up?'

" 'They become cats!' Tammy replied.

" 'That's right!' the magician said. 'And what do cats catch when they go hunting?'

" 'They catch birds,' Tammy answered.

"The magician shook his head. He bent over, wiggled his body pretending he was sniffing something. He looked here and there saying, 'Squeak, squeak, squeak.' He stretched one of his arms in back of him pretending it was a tail. He said in a high little squeaky voice, 'My name is Mickey . . . Mickey what?'

" 'Mouse!' Tammy said quickly.

"The magician nodded his head. He pulled the cloth off the bird cage and to everyone's surprise, the bird was gone. Instead, there was a little white mouse running around and around as if trying to find a way out of the cage.

"As the magician was folding his table and putting his magic things away Tammy asked him, 'Mr. Magician, can you change real, live lions into people?' She thought that if the lions in the circus were changed into people, she could play with them and have lots of fun.

"The magician stuck out his chest. 'Of course I can!'

"He raised his arms, looked up at the ceiling, and said some magic words. Then he told Tammy, 'Now all real, live lions have become people!' As he walked away, he looked back, saying, 'Don't be surprised if you see some real, live lions who didn't get changed into people. They weren't listening when I said my magic words.' Then he hurried away.

"After he left I asked Grandma how real, live lions who were far away could hear the magic words.

" 'Perhaps magic words go through the air like the words in a telephone do,' Grandma said.

"Tammy hoped that all the real, live lions at the circus had heard the magic words."

"Alice, it's getting past your bedtime. Don't you want me to finish the story tomorrow?" Grandma asked.

"No, no, Grandma," I begged her. "I want to hear the rest of the story now!"

"Alright," Grandma said, going on with the story.

"As soon as Tammy got home she told her

grandfather about the magician and that now she could play with the real, live lions because they had been changed into people who didn't have big teeth and claws. However, she didn't think it would be as much fun to play with them as if they had remained real, live lions.

"Her grandfather asked her, 'Do you really believe a magician can change lions into people?'

" 'Yes,' Tammy said. 'I saw him change a bird into a white mouse. Changing real, live lions into people isn't hard for him!' Then she asked her grandfather to phone the lion lady at the circus to ask her if her real, live lions had heard the magic words and had become people. He shook his head. He didn't want to do it.

"Tammy kept begging him to call the lion lady and ask her if her real, live lions had become people now. Grandfather knew that it was impossible for even the best magician in the world to change lions into people. But when he saw how much Tammy wanted him to call the lion lady in the circus, he agreed to phone her. After a while, they located the lion lady, and when she came to the phone she was so upset she could hardly speak.

" 'A terrible thing happened!' the lion lady told Tammy. 'All of my lions disappeared during the night. Instead, I found people sleeping in their cages this morning. What am I going to do?' she asked Tammy, and started to cry. She said, 'I'm going to lose my job. People don't come to my show to see people. They want to see real, live lions.' Then Tammy realized that she had been selfish in wanting real, live lions to become people. She hadn't thought of how the lion lady would feel.

" 'Don't cry, dear lion lady,' Tammy told her. 'I know how I can get the people who were in the cages changed back into real, live lions again!' she promised.

"The very next day Tammy asked her grand-father to help her find the magician. Her grand-father didn't want to look for him, but after he saw how sad Tammy was, he agreed, saying, 'Perhaps the walk would be good for me.'

"They looked for the magician all over town, but they couldn't find him anywhere. Just as they were about to return home, Tammy caught sight of the magician practicing his magic on a patio behind a big house.

" 'Oh, Mr. Magician!' Tammy called out to him. 'You must change the people who once were lions back into real, live lions again! Otherwise the lion lady will lose her job at the circus.'

"The magician thought that Tammy would never stop pestering him if he didn't do what she wanted. 'How can I undo what I did?' he asked himself aloud. Tammy held her breath waiting for him to think.

"Suddenly he said, 'Of course! I know how to do it! I'll say the same words I used before, only I'll say them backwards.' So he recited the magic words backwards. After he had finished, he turned to Tammy and said, 'It's done.' Tammy asked, 'Are all the people who used to be lions now real, live lions again?'

" 'Of course they are!' the magician replied frowning. 'Don't you think that if I can change lions into people, I can change people into lions?' Then he returned to practicing his magic tricks.

"When she got back home Tammy asked her grandfather to call the lion lady again. 'Are you glad to see that your real, live lions are back in their cages?' Tammy asked her when her grandfather gave her the receiver.

" 'Of course not!' she told Tammy. 'I don't believe a magician can change lions into people! Someone must have opened the doors to their cages and the lions ran out. Then some homeless people used the cages to sleep in. No people have been changed into real, live lions.' I have to go back to work now to practice my new job of balancing myself on the high wire that goes way over people's heads. It's much more fun than making lions do tricks.' "

"We have come to the end of the story,"

Grandma said. "The magician could change lions into people, but he couldn't change them back into real, live lions again. The people who were once good lions are now good people, but those who were bad lions are now bad people. They would hurt children if they could! You can't tell which one is good and which one is bad just by looking at them."

"That's why Tammy never went into anyone's car unless she knew the person. Her grandfather told her that only someone who had been a bad lion would ask children he didn't know to get into his car. Tammy never forgot that. Can you also remember it, Alice?"

"Yes, Grandma," I told her. She kissed me and said goodbye. That night I dreamed that the stuffed lion Grandma had given me was really a bad person pretending to be a good lion. When I woke up the next day Mom asked me if I remembered the story Grandma had told me.

"Oh, I do!" I said. "I'm sure that Tammy will never go into a car with a stranger. He might once have been a bad lion and would hurt her!"

Mother smiled and gave me a hug.

A few days later, I was walking alone as fast as I could to where the school bus stops to pick up us children. The lady that usually walks with me hadn't come. I hurried because I was afraid

I was going to be late. I saw the same car I'd seen before drive over to where I was walking. The man in the nice suit stopped his shiny blue car and said, ''Get in, little lady. I'll drive you to school so you won't be late.''

As I got into his car I thought he must have been a very good real, live lion before the magician turned him into a person.

Newspaper Headline:

PALMER GIRL FOUND

Alice Palmer was found by the police wandering along East County Road at 10 P.M., twelve miles from the city limits. Her clothes were torn, she was dazed and bruised as if she had been pushed out of a vehicle. The hospital confirmed that she had been sexually assaulted.

Alice described the perpetrator and his car with sufficient accuracy to enable the police to locate him. He is being held without bail while detectives are trying to tie him to several other molestations.

## COMMENT

*Grandma's story had charm. However, it failed to accomplish what it was intended to do. The story would have been more appropriate for a younger* child. Alice's behavior suggests that she may have been immature for her age. Six-year-old children may revert to behavior reminiscent of a two and one-half year old.

Alice's parents were overprotective in their wish not to frighten their daughter by pointing out to her, at an earlier age, the very real danger of going somewhere with a stranger. It is an unpleasant task to warn children that not every one can be trusted, but it is a necessary one. Perhaps her parents held back because of Alice's emotional immaturity which is shown by her behavior throughout the narrative. Alice's mother seemed to be insecure in her role as a parent and may have reinforced her daughter's immaturity. It would explain why she relied on her own mother to handle the problem instead of dealing with it herself.

Grandma's story would have been helpful and appropriate as an introduction to teaching a three-year-old child safe behavior when approached by a stranger. Children benefit from learning that one cannot always judge a book by it's cover, so to speak, and the lion story serves that goal without unnecessarily frightening a young child.

It is easy to see that, after they learned that their daughter was stopped as she was going to get into a stranger's car, her parents should have made ab-solutely certain that an adult would accompany her to the school bus. Additionally, they should have explained the danger of going with strangers and made sure that Alice understood it. Unfortunately, such parental oversights have led to many tragedies in the kind of a world we are living in today.

*After a year of counseling, Alice no longer experienced nightmares. During play therapy she was able to act out her anxieties and diffuse them. Her supportive family helped her regain a sense of self-worth. She was encouraged to participate in after-school activities and did so enthusiastically. Although some emotional scars will always remain, Alice was on the way to becoming the same happy child she had been before, with one exception—she lost interest in lions permanently.*

*Edith asked herself, "What could a first-grade teacher do about the racial strife that was making headlines in the newspaper?" Not much, she thought. "Nothing earthshaking" is the way the school psychologist put it. But anything that might help was worth trying, Edith decided. That afternoon while having her eyes tested for glasses, Edith had an idea.*

# EDITH:
# The Magic Glasses

"Lillian," I said to our school psychologist in the teachers' lounge as we finished our cups of decaf, "Did you see today's headline 'Racial Mix Boils Over'?"

"I saw it, Edith. But that's hardly news anymore, is it?" Lillian, who was African-American, replied.

"What can I do to help my first-grade children accept people of all races and ethnic groups without prejudice?" I asked her. In my mind I saw the toothless, smiling face of Lana, the little Korean girl my husband and I had adopted.

"I wish I knew what I could do besides lecturing with a lot of 'you shoulds' and 'you shouldn'ts,' " I told her.

Lillian nodded. She understood how I felt. "As you well know, reducing prejudice can't be accomplished by the schools single-handedly."

I could detect a trace of weariness in her voice. Who knows how many times she had gone over this same subject.

"Still, there are things we can do in our own small way by how we respond to children of different races and cultures in our classrooms," Lillian said. "No textbook can teach people how to feel in their heart. It's there that preventing prejudice must begin."

As Lillian gathered up her things she added, "Perhaps you can tell your first graders a story that could help them understand that diversity is what makes our world beautiful. With older children, one has to match wits. With children in the first grade one has to match imagination. That's why a story may be a good way to reach them. Your results won't be earthshaking, but you may do a little good in your own way."

I agreed, but wasn't sure I could find a story that would help my students appreciate human differences. If I could locate one in the library or make one up myself, how would my first-graders respond, I wondered.

Lillian glanced at her watch. "I have appointments and have to leave," she said. "Good luck in what you are trying to do."

The following day I went to an eye doctor to have my glasses checked. The doctor placed a number of different lenses in front of my eyes and told me to try to read the letters on the eye chart. Some of the letters were small and some were very large. Some lenses made the letters look clearer and others didn't. They all helped the doctor decide what kind of glasses I needed. As I thought about it, a story began to form in my mind. I was excited as I started to write the story that evening, and I worked late into the night to finish it.

The next day in class, I told the children, "I'm going to tell you a story." It was unusually quiet as twenty-three young faces looked up at me with expectation, eager to escape the usual routine.

"Will you try to remember the story all of your lives?" I asked, looking around the room at the upturned faces. The children nodded, eager for me to begin.

"In a small town there lived a man who tested people's eyes to find out if they needed to wear glasses. His name was Dr. Pult. He was a small man with white hair and a little white beard.

"Men, women, and children came to Dr. Pult from all around the countryside to have their eyes tested. He asked them to read letters, like A, B, C, on a chart that hung on the wall. The letters at the top of the chart were large, and others, at the bottom, were small. Dr. Pult told the people he tested to try to read the smallest letters they could. That was one of the ways he could tell if they needed glasses to see better.

"Dr. Pult always wanted to know what the world looked like through the glasses he made for other people. Before he gave anyone a new pair of glasses, he would put them on and look around his shop. He really couldn't see well through the glasses he had made for other people's eyes; when he looked through them everything was blurry. But he wouldn't think of giving anyone new glasses without trying them on himself first.

"One day a little girl named Linda came with her parents to Dr. Pult's shop to have her eyes tested. When Dr. Pult finished testing her eyes, he told Linda's parents that wearing glasses would help her see things more clearly. Linda's parents were glad because they wanted her to see everything as clearly as she could. Dr. Pult had lots of glasses to make, but promised to have Linda's ready the following week.

"A few days later, after Dr. Pult had finished making Linda's glasses, he held them in his hand and looked at them carefully. 'They are really beautiful glasses,' he said to himself as he admired them. 'They are the prettiest glasses I have ever made in my life.' He tried them on, but they pinched his nose because they were much too small for him. So he held them up to his eyes and looked through them as best he could. After one look through Linda's glasses, Dr. Pult put them down quickly. He blinked several times and then he picked the glasses up and looked through them again. He could hardly believe what he saw when he looked through the glasses he had made for Linda. For a long time he held them to his eyes and kept looking through them, frowning.

"Dr. Pult took a deep breath and tried to relax. He held the glasses to his eyes once more and looked around the room. Then he put the glasses down and rubbed his eyes to make sure he wasn't dreaming. Through Linda's glasses, nothing was the same color it had been before he put them on. *Everything* in the room was colored orange! As soon as he stopped looking through the glasses, everything was again the color it had been before.

"Hard as he tried, Dr. Pult couldn't explain it. He had made Linda's glasses exactly like the way he had made all the other glasses. Carefully he inspected the lenses. The glass he had used to make them didn't look orange at all. He held them up to the light that came through the window. The glasses were perfectly clear! Yet, when he had looked through them at the things in his shop, everything was colored orange like the color of the orange he had eaten for breakfast.

" 'Perhaps I'm seeing orange through the glasses because I have been working too hard,' he told himself. So he went home, got into bed, and went to sleep.

"The next morning, Dr. Pult woke up early. He had slept deeply, and now he felt fully refreshed. He could hardly wait to look through Linda's glasses again. As soon as he got to his shop, he ran right in, picked up Linda's glasses and looked through them.

"For a long time he looked around the shop, holding Linda's glasses to his eyes and breathing hard. Yes, again everything he looked at had a beautiful orange color. But during the night something even stranger had happened. When Dr. Pult looked through the glass now, all the same kinds of things were exactly the same shape and size!

"Dr. Pult went into his workshop next to his office holding Linda's glasses to his eyes and looked around. The little screwdrivers he used to tighten the lenses into their frames and the big ones he used to build his cabinets, were exactly the same size. And the different hammers all were the same size and shape. And they all were orange colored.

"Dr. Pult went into the waiting room of his shop and held the glasses to his eyes once more. All the small pictures had grown bigger and the big pictures had grown smaller. They all covered exactly the same amount of space on the wall! All of the chairs were the same height! But worst of all, the very worst thing that could have happened, was that when he looked at the eye chart—the chart he used for testing people's eyesight—all the letters were exactly the same size! 'Oh, how will I ever test people's eyes again?' he asked himself, becoming very upset.

"Quickly, he took the glasses off and looked around. Immediately, the big pictures were again big and the little pictures were small. Best of all, the little letters on the eye chart were little again and the big letters were big. In his workshop his tools again were their real sizes, shapes, and color.

"In all of his life, Dr. Pult had never had such a problem. He knew that in a few days Linda would come to his shop to get her glasses. He decided to make another pair of glasses for her as quickly as he could. This time he wanted to be very careful and make sure he didn't use orange-colored glass or any other kind of glass different from what he usually used to make glasses.

"After Dr. Pult had finished making the new glasses, he could hardly wait to look through them. He was very much afraid that everything would look orange as it had when he looked through the first pair of glasses he had made for Linda.

"To his relief, the new glasses were just like all the other glasses he had always made. When he held them up to his eyes, he found that only those things looked orange that really were orange, like the marigold flowers in the clay pot on his desk. Carefully, he looked around everywhere and saw that all things had the shapes and sizes they should have. The second pair of glasses weren't at all like the strange ones he had made for Linda before.

"Dr. Pult was glad he had the new glasses ready when Linda and her parents came to his shop. He smiled when he saw how happy Linda was when she put them on and could see everything much clearer than before. Just as Linda and her parents were getting ready to leave, Dr. Pult took the first, strange glasses out of a drawer. 'Would you like to try these on?' he asked.

"Linda put them on and caught her breath. All the different colors in the room had changed into a beautiful orange color. It made her think of how the world looked when it was colored golden orange by a large evening sun setting low in the sky. It was even more surprising that all the chairs she looked at were the same size and shape, and the tables also were all the same size and shape. But what surprised Linda most was that her father, who was tall and thin, and Dr. Pult, who was short and chubby, now were exactly the same size and shape. And both of them had skin that was the color of ripe oranges that grow on trees.

" 'Oh, these are magic glasses!' Linda cried out with delight. 'The world is more beautiful when I look at it through these magic glasses!' She was so happy, that she danced around the room singing, 'I love to see everything in the whole world dressed in a beautiful orange color. Things look so neat and straight when they are the same size and shape. Please let me keep the magic glasses,' she begged her parents. 'I like them much better than the other ones!'

"Before Linda's parents would let her keep the strange glasses they looked through them themselves. To their surprise, they saw that all the things in Dr. Pult's shop looked so much alike, it made them think of soldiers wearing orange uniforms marching in a parade. Linda's father and mother exchanged looks and shook their heads. They didn't want Linda to wear glasses that turned all the different colors into only one color, and made all things of the same kind look exactly alike. But hard as they tried, they couldn't convince Linda to choose the glasses that would let her see the world as it really was.

" 'Oh, how wonderful the whole world looks through my new magic glasses!' Linda said when she put them on again. She begged her parents to let her wear them. She wanted them so much that, at last, they agreed to let her keep them.

"After Linda left Dr. Pult's shop with her parents, she looked around through her new glasses and saw that all the houses on the street looked exactly alike. Yes, and all the people looked alike. All the children looked like little twins and the grown-ups looked like grown-up twins. How marvelous these glasses are, Linda thought, feeling very happy and excited.

"For the next few weeks, everything Linda saw through her glasses delighted her. But her parents began to notice that, sometimes, Linda took the magic glasses off just to see what the world really looked like. After a while, Linda began to tire of seeing everything in just one color. She wanted to see the red cheeks of the apples her mother gave her to eat. She wanted to see flowers in their real colors—blue and green and red, as well as orange. Dr. Pult had told Linda's parents that it would be best for Linda to wear her glasses all the time so she wouldn't strain her eyes. Therefore, her parents wouldn't let her take her glasses off very often.

"Linda used to be a happy girl, but as time went by, she became the saddest girl in the whole town. She found that she couldn't have much fun when so many things looked alike and everything was the same color. More than anything, Linda now wanted to see tall grass and small grass, big trees and little trees, black horses, white horses, brown horses, and horses whose colors were all mixed up.

"She didn't want to see orange kittens that were the same size and shape as their orange mother cat. She longed to see fat people and thin people, tall people and short people, people with dark skin and light skin.

"How terrible it was, she thought, that when she wore her magic glasses, all of her dresses looked exactly alike. And her shoes looked alike! And all of the mountains in the distance were the same height. And every dog looked like every other dog. And her house looked like every other house!

"Things were meant to look different, Linda thought. All rivers weren't meant to be the same length. All mountains weren't meant to be the same height. All trees weren't meant to have the same kind of leaves. People's eyes and hair weren't meant to look exactly alike. She knew now that it was the different way things looked that helped make the world beautiful! With that, she took off her magic glasses and threw them away as far as she could. She watched them disappear in the tall grass. She hoped that no one would ever find them.

"Linda couldn't see clearly without glasses, but she could tell that there were different colors all around her, and that things no longer looked alike. She sang:

> I'm happy when I look around
>
> Without wearing magic glasses!
>
> Our eyes were made to see
>
> The different shapes and colors
>
> That make the world beautiful!

"Did Linda get a scolding when her parents saw that she wasn't wearing her magic glasses?

"No. When they saw her happy face, her father and mother were glad that she no longer was wearing them. They took her right back to Dr. Pult's shop. When he saw Linda he smiled. 'I have saved the other glasses for you,' he told her. 'I was sure you would come back to get them.'

" 'Some people,' Dr. Pult said, shaking his head, 'want everyone to wear magic glasses all of their lives.'

"Linda was sad when she heard this. 'I feel sorry for them,' she said. 'They don't know that people weren't meant to all look alike.' Then she put on the glasses Dr. Pult had saved for her. She looked around and saw the world as it was really meant to be. Now Linda was happy again.''

Edith's eyes swept over the children's faces. How many of her first-graders had gotten her message. Had her story influenced any of them—even a little bit? She doubted it, but when she saw how thoughtful the children looked, and how quiet they were, she had hope.

"How many of you would like to wear Linda's magic glasses?" she asked the class. To her disappointment, three small hands shot up immediately.

"You, Henry?" she pointed to the red-haired, freckle-faced boy who had been endearingly mischievous all year.

"Yes," Henry said eagerly. "I'd want to see what things would look like through the magic glasses. Then I'd take them right off again!" Black and brown faces that went with the other raised hands nodded in agreement.


## COMMENT

*Would children be more inclined to accept physical differences after listening to Edith's story? Some children probably would. Edith had planted a seed in her first-graders' minds that, depending on their life experiences, might grow into an acceptance of human differences. The children in Edith's class may have felt that their teacher's intentions came from her heart, where Lillian had said prevention of prejudice must begin. In their hearts people know that beneath physical differences there are the same human fears, feelings, and hopes.*

Sometimes a dramatic event shocks a person into giving up false perceptions of people of a different culture or ethnicity. This is what happened to Eric, whose story was told in this book. There is no doubt that human nature can be shaped by example and education, enabling children to accept and appreciate human differences if conditions permit it.

Our world is rich in human diversity, and every year people all over the world are drawn closer together by the spread of modern technology. Nevertheless, within every group there are people who claim that they know how to make ours a better world. Some of these people are wearing Linda's magic glasses. Can they succeed? Most certainly not, especially, if they don't even know they have them on!

## APPENDIX

### POINTS TO PONDER

In the book the narrators describe their encounters with their therapists and with family members involved in their problems. The stories by and about children illustrate their reactions to adults attempting to modify their behavior. The following may be used as topics for discussions:

1. Pete: Occasionally a patient has an experience occurring outside of the therapeutic setting that plays a role in the outcome of the therapy. If the therapist is unaware of it he or she may, inadvertently, believe that the therapy was responsible for consequences of the event. This is one of several reasons why it is sometimes difficult to evaluate the results of therapy.

2. Wilhelmina: Cures may have short-lived hazards that neither the patient nor the therapist anticipate. As the patient changes, the world around the patient changes.

3. Walter: Sometimes mental patients discharged from a hospital treatment program become separated from their court-appointed supervisors. If these patients strike out on their own, there may be unpredictable consequences.

4. Lisa and Helen: In contrast to sexual abuse, sexual harassment in childhood is seldom brought to light. Childhood sexual harassment and exposure to different parental values

can lead to a personality split and to inner conflicts later in life.

5. Henry: Hypochondriacs do not "fake" their symptoms even though their complaints have no physical bases. Preoccupation with imagined medical problems stems from anxiety converted into obsessive health concern.

6. Gladys: Sociological and psychological factors are interrelated in creating mental disorders. Prejudice often has an economic basis.

7. Anne and Joan: During a terminal illness, or after the death of a loved one, membership in a support group may help a person cope with mixed-up feelings that could precipitate a catastrophic reaction. Sharing feelings with people having similar experiences is effective preventative therapy.

8. Bill: People with passive aggressive personalities are usually not good subjects for hypnotic intervention. If they are hypnotized, their covert resistance may show up later in their response to a posthypnotic suggestion.

9. Eric: Violent prejudice against people of a different race, ethnicity, or religion, tends to be destructive to all concerned. Tolerance and acceptance are society's healers.

10. Sharon: A therapist who betrays a patient's trust creates deep emotional scars that are even more devastating if they reactivate a previous betrayal of trust.

11. Carol: Mental health do-it-yourself efforts usually fail when they are applied by a person who has a history of severe emotional trauma.

12. Tom: A psychologist experienced in testing can detect malingering almost every time.

13. Freddy: The conflicting emotions that parents of a mentally retarded child may experience can create disruptive family problems. Special schools and social work agencies are located in most communities to serve as resources to such families.

14. Tommy: Former role models continue to exert influence with an invisible, guiding hand.

15. Jim: There is seldom a mystery behind mass murder if one realizes that the murderer is obsessed by the idea that life has been unfair to him and that he sees his victims as symbols of people who have wronged him.

16. Jayson: Even with the best of intentions it is usually futile to try to impose one's own values on persons conditioned by different life experiences.

17. Douglas: The gamut of emotions experienced by people who have a terminal disease do not always follow each other in the sequence described in textbooks. Disaster often unites people who would not even notice each other before it occurred.

18. Mervin/Mary: The more anxious a person is during self-evaluation, the more the person is apt to miss seeing the obvious.

19. Melissa: Biochemical and genetic factors are now believed to play a role in eating disorders that previously were thought to have been caused solely by events from the person's environment.

20. Karen: At the termination of therapy, a patient's action, off-hand remark, or fleeting look may incline a therapist to reevaluate the success of the patient's treatment despite the apparent remission of the patient's symptoms.

21. Michelle: Some parents fail to notice the danger signals of suicide given them by their children or are unaware of their seriousness. Yet suicide is a leading cause of death among teenage children.

22. Ralph: When youngsters who are in trouble look back into their past, they are likely to find only self-justification. Preventing child delinquency by comprehensive early childhood intervention is a promising new approach.

23. Cindy and Me: Unanticipated problems often follow a divorce. Children may show unexpected loyalty to the non-custodial divorced parent, be overloaded with responsibility, and fail to accept a stepparent.

24. Alice: Warning a child of potential danger by using story-telling may not give the child

a clear enough message. Such warnings must take into account the child's level of understanding and should be followed by reminders and supervision.

25. Edith: Story-telling is often helpful in shaping children's social attitudes.

Some time in the future, after the human genome is mapped, geneticists could become potential Dr. Pults who might be tempted to provide us with genetically designed "Magic Glasses" we couldn't take off. Before we let them do this, let's ask them to consult Linda.

The story applies equally to cultural and psychological differences among people. These also help to make the world beautiful.